FROM SOPHOCLES TO PICASSO

The Present-day Vitality of the Classical Tradition

(*verso*)
Etruscan Figurine, early V cent. B.C.,
bronze

FROM

The Present-day Vitality
of the Classical Tradition
—
edited by **WHITNEY J. OATES**

Indiana University Press / *Bloomington*

SOPHOCLES TO PICASSO

On pages 71-118, figures 7, 8, 9, 11, 12, 13, 15, and 16 have been reproduced from volumes of *Picasso* by Christian Zervos by permission of the
publishers, Cahiers d'art (Paris); figures 1 and 3 from L. Goldscheider,
Leonardo da Vinci, courtesy Phaidon Press Ltd. (London); figure 6 from
L. Venturi, *Cézanne: Son Art—Son Oeuvre* by permission of Paul Rosenberg
and Co.; figure 14 from J. M. C. Toynbee, *The Hadrianic School,* by permission of The University Press (Cambridge, England); and figure 20 from
Verve magazine by permission of the publisher. On pages 121-159, figures
4 and 10 have been reproduced from Zervos's *Picasso* by permission of the
publisher. Figures 1, 2, 3, 5, and 9 in the same article have been reproduced
by permission of The Museum of Modern Art, New York; figures 4 and 7 in
the previous article are by permission of the Museum. The Metropolitan
Museum of Art provided the illustration on page 37, from its collection. The
Press is also grateful to Mr. Curtis O. Baer, Mr. Norbert Schimmel, M.
Knoedler and Co., the Metropolitan Museum of Art, and Indiana University
Fine Arts Department for permission to reproduce several works from their
collections.

Works in the Picasso collection have been reproduced by permission of
SPADEM, © 1962 by French Reproduction Rights, Inc.

Financial assistance towards publication was provided by the American
Council of Learned Societies.

TABLE OF CONTENTS

ILLUSTRATIONS

FROM SOPHOCLES TO PICASSO

The Present-day Vitality of the Classical Tradition

(*verso*)
Head of a Young Woman, Greek,
  IV-early II cent. B.C., marble

Whitney J. Oates

FOR ALL scholars and intelligent laymen in this country, the renaissance of the American Council of Learned Societies some years ago was an event of exceptional significance. Not only humanists but also individuals concerned primarily with other aspects of the life of the mind realized that here was a fresh opportunity to help create a fruitful balance among the learned activities of the nation. In such a spirit the Board of Directors of the Council decided that normally thereafter it would devote some portion of its annual meeting to a scrutiny of the subject matter of one or more of its constituent societies, not only to publicize this material more widely but also, when appropriate, to underscore its contemporary relevance. In January of 1957 the focus of attention fell upon the eighteenth century and in the following year the theme selected was "The Present-day Vitality of the Classical Tradition." This book in part contains the record of a truly memorable program or, one might better say, demonstration, which was offered to the Council, its guests, and the community on the campus of Indiana University.

Those of us whose responsibility it became to design the program were deeply aware of the numerous difficulties to be confronted. Above all, the Classical Tradition is so manifold and does possess so many facets that any thought of "covering" it within the short time available was out of the question. Hence it was necessary to meet the problem by selecting some point or basic focus that would illustrate with maximum immediacy the general contention that the Classical Tradition is indeed profoundly vital in the world of the mid-twentieth century. Students of the history of Western culture and civilization know that each succeeding epoch has singled out one or another aspect of the Classical Tradition as particularly significant. For example, during the early centuries of the development of Christianity, the philosophical views of Plato, Aristotle, and the Stoics stimulated the minds and hearts of those who were destined to mold the future of this new religion. Or again, the rediscovery of the Classics in the Renaissance affected broadly the arts and letters of the period, and produced a philosophical undergirding in the *Weltanschauung* of Humanism.

The eighteenth century reacted most strongly to the political insights of antiquity, while in the nineteenth century we are familiar with the varying ways in which the Classical Tradition spurred the imaginations of such men as Keats, Shelley, and Matthew Arnold.

What element, then, in this incredibly rich cultural heritage can be identified as the one to which our own century has been peculiarly responsive? The essays and addresses here offered argue either directly or by implication that this element is the Greek sense of tragedy. Everyone knows that Tragedy is the creation of the Greeks. And everyone knows, for example, how often our contemporary dramatists have sought their inspiration from Greek tragedy. One need only mention Eugene O'Neill's *Mourning Becomes Electra* or T. S. Eliot's *The Family Reunion*, both of which depend from the *Oresteia*, the masterwork of Aeschylus. Striking corroborative evidence for the transcendental significance of the Greek tragic sense in our age will be found in Roger Sessions' essay on music. There he demonstrates that, whereas eighteenth and nineteenth century composers rarely turned to the Classics for theme or idea, many of our contemporary composers, both young and old, have looked to the Classics for their stimulus, and have found it precisely in that Greek tragic sense. Notable is Igor Stravinsky's *Oedipus Rex*.

The basic method or technique employed for the "demonstration" of the thesis consisted in the confrontation of ancient and contemporary matching works of art. Hence, after Professor Eric Havelock's opening explanation of the program, a concert reading of Sophocles' *Antigone* was presented in the great auditorium of Indiana University by a professional Broadway cast assembled with the cooperation of the American National Theatre and Academy. There followed immediately a full-dress production of the modern French adaptation of the play by Jean Anouilh in the adjoining smaller theatre, the players in this instance being students in the University's drama department. Here we must emphatically recommend that, if one is to recreate successfully the experience of the demonstration, he should read consecutively the texts of Sophocles and Anouilh after having finished Havelock's essay.

This opening phase of the program occupied an evening. A word here about the selection of Sophocles' *Antigone* as the most illuminating Greek tragedy for the occasion. In the first place, there are two tragic characters, for the play portrays not only the tragedy of Antigone, but also the tragedy of her opponent, Creon. Furthermore, political issues are raised, and in this respect an additional dimension of the Classical Tradition is introduced over and above the tragic sense. Finally, the version of Anouilh, written for production in Paris during the German occupation in World War II, illustrates one of the variety of ways in which a Greek tragedy may be adapted with success to a different time and a different place. For these various reasons Sophocles' *Antigone* seemed a singularly effective instrument for the communication of the Greek sense of tragedy. As Professor

Kitto has observed, the adaptations or progeny of Greek tragedy are legion, whereas there have been no adaptations of the less concentrated, more discursive masterpieces of Shakespeare, such as *Othello, Lear,* or *Hamlet.*

Before considering the next phases of the demonstration, which took place on the following day, it is important to underscore the role played by the exhibition of painting and sculpture which had been mounted with great skill be the staff of the University's Department of Fine Arts in the spacious foyer of the auditorium. Here likewise the method of confrontation was invoked by juxtaposing an ancient art object and a modern counterpart. The purpose, of course, was in no sense an attempt to prove that the ancient "prototype" specifically "influenced" the modern example. Rather, the effort was to show by direct comparison how the classical object, in theme or motif or subject matter or content, by its very vitality or livingness has found re-expression in a variety of ways in modern sculpture and painting. Furthermore, since it was intended that the program should expose the audience to the maximum possible extent to works of art, whether of drama, painting, sculpture, or music, the precise location of the exhibition was of primary importance. As two of the formal sessions took place in the auditorium, each member of the audience passed through the "museum" in the foyer at least four times. Many persons took other opportunities to study the exhibition more carefully. It well repaid further examination, for all the objects, ancient and modern, were originals, assembled not only from the holdings of Indiana University but also from other museums and private collections.

The context for the work of the second day had been established in these several ways so that Professor H. D. F. Kitto faced an audience which had been immediately in contact with specimens of ancient and modern tragedy, and ancient and modern art. In his masterful analysis of Sophocles' *Antigone* he compares and contrasts it with other Sophoclean plays, with Shakespearean tragedy, and with the version of Anouilh. Particularly striking is Kitto's identification of the principle of concentration in Greek tragedy as the most potent means whereby the Greek tragic sense is communicated in all its intensity.

After a brief interval, the demonstration shifted sharply to the medium of contemporary painting. No doubt many were puzzled when they saw in their program that Professor Otto Brendel of Columbia University was to lecture on "Classic and Non-Classic Elements in Picasso's Guernica Painting." How in any sense could this painting be used to support the thesis that the Classical Tradition is perennially vital? Professor Brendel, whose scholarship as an art historian is distinguished in the two fields of ancient art and modern painting, argued his cause with striking vividness as will be apparent when the reader studies the text of his address along with its accompanying illustrations. Quite apart from the palpable "non-classic" elements in the *Guernica* painting, Dr. Brendel showed how, both in form and in content, the power of the Classical Tradition was in fact operating in the construction of the Picasso masterpiece. Dr. Brendel strongly emphasizes the demonic element in the Classics.* In underscoring the demonic, he indicates that in a most profound sense the tragedy of the *Guernica* painting derives from its ancient forebear. In order to support more broadly Brendel's thesis, a second essay, not presented at the meeting but which he has kindly made available, has been included in this volume. Entitled "The Classical Style in Modern Art," this article submits additional wide-ranging evidence that makes even more compelling his contention that the Classical Tradition has pervaded the whole area of modern art.

The next session of the demonstration heard the testimony of the contemporary painter, Stephen Greene, who described the powerful influence that the Greek tragic sense had exerted on his own work. Professor Herbert J. Muller of Indiana University followed with his lecture, "Freedom and the Classical Tradition." It served to remind the audience that we have inherited other aspects of the Greek tradition which, besides the tragic sense, lie at the heart of our contemporary culture. Such, of course, is the idea of freedom itself, and Professor Muller has made abundantly clear how the idea originated and how it has been transmitted to us. I am adding here

---

* This point has been ably elucidated by Professor E. R. Dodds in his recent book, *The Greeks and the Irrational* (Berkeley, 1951).

to the evidence submitted by Muller a memorable quotation from Herodotus's account of the Persian Wars, when the Greeks successfully defended their freedom against foreign attack. Early in the work (III. 80) Herodotus declares for democracy, saying,

How could monarchy be a well-ordered thing, where the ruler can do what he will and not be called to account for it? For indeed the best of all men, once in such a position would be set outside the ordinary thoughts. For insolence grows in him out of the blessings he has. . . . But the rule of the many (i.e., democracy)—first, its name is of all most beautiful, to wit, *isonomy*, equality before the law; and next it does none of the things that a monarch does. The offices are assigned by lot; no man has rule without being accountable; and it carries all counsels to the general assembly.

T. R. Glover comments on this passage in these eloquent words:

Herodotus sees in the progress of Athens after the attainment of liberty a proof of Freedom's value. He knows what men say of Democracy,—how much easier it is to humbug a multitude than one man, how jealous the vulgar are of one another,—the violence of a useless mob, its insolence worse than the insolence of a tyrant because less informed, its ignorance of what is best and its unwillingness to learn, its headlong sweep—into business without reflection. Yet liberty, equality, fraternity, in spite of the crimes done in their name are beautiful things, as he says. Herodotus sticks to the most daring of all faiths, that at bottom you can trust the people. Athens grew great on Freedom; and, grown great, she above all others saved the Freedom of all the Greeks, and he loves her above all other Greek cities, as we all do.*

* *Herodotus* (Berkeley, 1924), p. 220.

Professor Havelock then returned to the stage in the role of epiloguist and with skill, wit, and high seriousness summarized the whole demonstration, closing his remarks with a moving quotation from Abraham Lincoln. A final event, conceived as a musical *envoi*, remained. Once more the audience passed through the art exhibition into the auditorium. After the introductory remarks by Roger Sessions, performances of several contemporary compositions were presented by the students and faculty of the Indiana University School of Music. Outstanding was the setting of a chorus of Sophocles' *Oedipus Tyrannus* by Seymour Shifrin. Given a masterful rendition, the chorus clearly emphasized that quintessential element of the Classical Tradition, the Greek sense of tragedy. In this way the case made by drama, criticism, painting, and sculpture was completed by music.

The foregoing pages have attempted to recreate the experience of the meeting, but the present volume should be, and indeed is, more than the record of an extraordinary and fascinating event. For the reader interested in and concerned with the nature of the Classics and the great tradition which emerged therefrom, the essays provide striking evidence of the scope and richness of that tradition. For example, the papers by Otto Brendel indicate how pervasively the classical spirit in its many-sidedness has penetrated the creative activity of modern art. And at the same time, within this broad scope, there is the intensity of the focus on the tragic so powerfully communicated in the *Guernica* painting. Similarly, Professor Muller's concentration on the concept of freedom, as we have already noted, calls attention to this all-important element in our classical inheritance as another indication of its scope. Indeed Sophocles' *Antigone* more than adequately attests that freedom itself cannot be dissociated from the tragic.

Somone may be tempted to define the Classical Tradition. This seems to us impossible, as it is always impossible to define the ultimate and all-embracing. The Classical holds within itself the rational and the irrational, reason and mysticism, humanism and profound theology, serenity and violence, joy and despair. To repeat a point already made, it is no wonder that each age or epoch has discovered in this comprehensiveness an element to which it peculiarly responds. So there is a sense in which each age or epoch distinctively defines or describes itself by its choice of the element within the Classical with which it feels itself to be most compatible. If this contention be accepted, then, as the present volume urges, our own century has in a radical way characterized itself by reacting as it has to the Greek tragic sense. To complete our argument: if the tragic sense or view constitutes a profound, if not the most profound, reading of the human condition ever to appear in history, then our century, despite all its superficial chaos, may achieve a depth of sensitivity and vision which will enable us to face our future and to overcome it with courage, with dignity, and with hope—with all those powers that befit man.

Etruscan Votive Statuette,
VI cent. B.C., bronze, (7½″ high)

Eric A. Havelock

P UBLIC OPINION in the United States has shown an increasing tendency to accept the proposition that our North American culture is autonomous, or at least that it ought to be. This concept, though originally promoted by certain of our historians and philosophers, has become popularized today as a form of loyalty to the American way of life in which we are all supposed to share. Accordingly the revolution which separated us politically from Europe has seemed to require that in the course of time we demonstrate our independence in other areas besides politics, such as literature and the arts and education and industrial techniques, and finally in a kind of moral outlook which is supposed to reflect a freedom and independence native to our shores.

It is probable, however, that an observer from Mars, were he to descend upon our planet and undertake a survey of its inhabitants, as he came to consider the communities that border on both sides of the Atlantic ocean, would be more struck by their similarities than their differences. Is it not still to be admitted that in essential respects—in our language, our politics, our religion, our law, our values and even some of our prejudices—we remain Europeans? This is not to say that the development of varieties within the European pattern and the adaptation of what we have inherited is not a proper American task. The pursuit of excellence is always specific, not general, and the differences in style and emphasis which divide us from Europe are not less real and meaningful for being subtle.

But in these days, as the foreign policies of our government become increasingly enmeshed with those of our European partners, and as we find ourselves not only shouldering responsibilities for the welfare of peoples on the other side of the Atlantic but also to some extent becoming involved in their fate, it is appropriate to turn away a while from the contemplation of our Americanism in order to consider our traditional roots in a not-so-remote past. The civilization of our European partners was not itself an entirely home-grown product of northern Europe. It had its own roots in the countries bordering on the Mediterranean basin. Mesopotamia, Egypt, Crete, and Anatolia all took an early hand in our shaping; but we may say a stamp of finality was set by Greece, if we add that it was a stamp engraved upon the mind and spirit of our civilization. For Rome was reserved the task of setting in order the outward man: we live not alone by intellect and spirit but also by institutions and legalities and material order.

In the long progress of the generations we seem today to enjoy a distinction which is unique and uncomfortable. We have an ancestry, but is it equally certain that we shall have descendants? We have taken our place in the long relay race run by civilized man, but by the time we have accomplished our course will there be any survivors to whom the torch while still alight can be transmitted? Thoughtful men now ponder this problem in the face of what seems to be an admitted fact—that our culture has devised a means for destroying itself, and may still use it. In these dangerous days there is profit in looking back over the course we have been running. If we do, we shall discover for one thing that the threat and the fact of destruction is not new. The archaeologist can always find more ruins. Sumer and Babylon, the Cretan kings and the Egyptian dynasts—where are they? This at first sight seems rather negative consolation, unless it be true that the scholar who slowly and painfully recreates the vestiges of a vanished culture, adding item to item in his accumulating list, is also teaching us to tame our pride and to temper our own decisions in the light—as we say—of history.

If, however, we look back only as far as Greece, we gain a keener sense of immediacy and learn a livelier set of lessons, not simply because Greece is a little nearer to us in time but because the Greeks spoke with a still-living voice. We know their language and can still hear what they actually said, thanks to the record which was guarded for our benefit through later antiquity and the Middle Ages. What can the spoken accents of Greece still declare that will be relevant to our own present dilemma? Can they declare anything relevant at all?

I think they can. Of all the themes proclaimed and sung by the poets and writers of Athens, one now begins to sound dominant. It is the theme of the tragic experience as that experience was raised to a high and serious level by the dramatists of the Athenian stage. The Greeks could laugh and make merry with the rest of mankind; they could fight heroically, debate passionately; they could make love with fervor, and reason with cool precision. But at bottom they were conscious of the human dilemma. They knew that man's course is complicated, his decisions dangerous, and his destiny ambiguous. The Greek city-states of the classical period were the constant targets of all the vicissitudes that nature, fortune, and human violence can bring. The private citizen lived frugally on the edge of want, competing with his fellows and with his environment by land and sea in ceaseless enterprise, but also uncertainty.

It was given to certain poets of Athens to look these facts in the face in a mood neither defiant nor despairing. They found the resources, within a traditional mythology and expressed in a superb language, to achieve a grand summary of the human dilemma. They were able to present man at the peak of his energy with all his drives, his fears, his purposes and passions, his errors and triumphs, his endurance and his defeat. They did this dispassionately but with a certain underlying compassion which is not confined to the heroes at the expense of the villains; for there are no heroes and villains, just as it is hard to find them in our own historical experience.

The classical tradition considered as a whole has to be something we look back to. Otherwise it would not be a tradition. But looking back is not a simple operation. The post-classical world, whenever it has resorted to contemplation of Greece and Rome, in art, literature or politics, has done so to find there some image of itself. This essentially is why looking back is worthwhile. It is done not to copy or repeat but to reselect and re-create, and there is some evidence—which American historians and sociologists would do well to note—that unless you have something to look back to, even if only in hostility, the act of creation does not take place. Cultural processes are organic and if you interrupt them you cannot start precisely where you left off. You descend in the scale of human energy and achievement before you start again.

To recreate, as I have said, is also to reselect. In the literature of antiquity there are many themes to choose from and many types of achievement with which our sympathetic imagination may identify. In earlier periods of the European experience, and even in the comparatively recent history of America, we would probably not have chosen the masque of tragedy as the mirror of contemporary mood. The very term classic, suggesting as it does what is ideal and therefore monolithic, serves too often to hide from us the astonishing variety and even the contradictions within the complex experience of the men of Greece and Rome. Here in the classic monuments are statements on life, tragic and comic, pastoral and lyric, philosophic and legal. In the Renaissance it was chiefly the classical artist who beckoned in the formal beauties of written word and plastic form. Shakespeare found there, to be sure mainly in translation, the grandeur and dignity of great men and large events. The eighteenth century embraced the control and decorum and elegance of Roman oratory and poetry. The Romantics, devoted to a creed of passionate sensibility, perceived the white arm of the nymph raised in the waterfall. The British governing class in the latter part of the nineteenth century could derive from Aristotle a conception of practical wisdom suitable to mold the moral character of administrators and statesmen. It is pertinent in this connection to recall the remarks of Alfred North Whitehead on the subject of his classical schooling:

We read Latin and Greek as the historical records of governing peoples who had lived close to the sea and exerted maritime power. They were not foreign languages; they were just Latin and Greek; nothing of importance in the way of ideas could be presented in any other way. Thus we read the New Testament in Greek. At school—except in Chapel which did not count—I never heard of anyone reading it in English. It would suggest an uncultivated religious state of mind. We were religious but with that moderation natural to people who take their religion in Greek.*

* *Dialogues of Alfred North Whitehead* (Boston, 1954), p. 5.

This reminiscence illuminates the complicated and diverse character of the classical experience. That experience has almost everything. Its students in each epoch can, by an exercise of unconscious selection, find that aspect which is relevant to their own situation. Where the Renaissance saw beauty, the late Victorian British found political science.

Let us return then to the proposition already stated. It would appear that we, at this point of time, having entered the last half of the twentieth century, should desire to look at classical antiquity with some relevance to our own situation. If we want to look for courage or comfort or understanding or just plain sympathy for our own reflection, we shall find it just now not in the Pax Romana and the age of the Antonines, nor in the confident and polished periods of Cicero, nor in the timeless forms of Platonism, nor even in the simple heroics of Homer, but on the dramatic stage of Periclean Athens. The watchword is not decorum but danger.

Whether we pursue the ever-receding goals of power and success, or simply accept as a matter of routine the rather easy motions that an affluent society requires of us, we have become aware that our condition of euphoria has its undercurrent of private uneasiness and its memories of public catastrophe. Some of our sons for example— I speak here to the older among us—are no longer with us and others have had to face dislocation or danger before being allowed to enter the ranks of civil life. The beaches of Okinawa and Normandy and the mountains of Korea have taken their toll. Nor in the context of world events is it only Americans who have carried the burden of history. Great cities to the east and the west of us have been devastated, and villages of comfort have been laid waste. Though our own soil has been spared, we may comprehend the fate of mother cities of Europe and Japan, and if we do, we may comprehend also that there is abroad in the world a kind of litany which in many places celebrates the forceful assault and the violent breach that takes so much away, destroys so much. This can be done more easily in Greek than in our own chopped speech. It comes more naturally to us through the medium of a chorus such as the one sung in the *Hecuba* of Euripides:

> Thou O Ilium my country and my home
> Shalt no longer be called the city of the undespoiled;
> Such a cloud of the enemy covers thee over: with
>   sword and with spear have they ravished thee—
> Shorn of all thy coronal of towers,
> Stained with the smoke and the smear of burning—
> Alas nevermore shall I haunt thy streets again.

Two world wars within the span of a generation have added their own relevance to these lines. So speaks the exile, the displaced person, the inheritor of the cosmopolis of Hellas. The modern imagination, speaking through familiar lines in *The Waste Land*, has repeated the theme:

> What is that sound high in the air
> Murmur of maternal lamentation
> Who are those hooded hordes swarming
> Over endless plains stumbling in cracked earth
> Ringed by the flat horizon only

What is the city over the mountains
Cracks and reforms and bursts in the violet air
Falling towers
Jeruslem, Athens, Alexandria
Vienna, London.*

We may say then that this is part of the regular business of the Tragic Muse—to lament. It is almost routine. It is this that purges us and strengthens us and keeps us honest. Such catastrophes must be accepted for what they are, passionately and completely, in protest and abnegation, not glossed over with moral commonplace or just forgotten in the business of parking our car at the shopping center. Picasso's famous representation of the destruction of Guernica is faithful to this classic function.

But the span of experience and feeling measured in Greek tragedy is far wider than this. The Tragic Muse is not simply and narrowly tragic in the modern and pathetic sense of the word. Grief is there but only in the conclusion, and even then it is relevant only as it becomes also an act of understanding. What is understood and finally accepted is not a moral tale or a platitude. The vision is more complicated. The Tragic Muse is not fatalistic or submissive, even though her instrument, the chorus, may be both. She is the whole of the play, and in the play the plot and the characters become the instruments for perceiving and penetrating to the *modus operandi* which brings about such negative results from such positive motives. The solutions to this puzzle do not depend upon pitting stage villain against hero or

---

* T. S. Eliot, "The Waste Land," *Collected Poems* (New York, 1952), ll. 366-375.

heroine. The Muse is less judgmental, and perhaps less Christian, more historical and more ultimately dispassionate. Over and over again on the stage of Athens she offers us the irresistible force confronted by the immovable object. The antithesis becomes almost a law of human behavior—how things are arranged and how they turn out. It is the tragic law. This is the secret of the disasters of mankind. If they would only hold back from the ultimate assertion. When the argument is all over, neither side has won a moral victory which is unqualified. Life does not fall into such neat patterns. It does not matter whether the antagonists who put in their claims for moral decision are Antigone and Creon, or Oedipus and Apollo, or the triangle of Hippolytus and Phaedra and Theseus. They plead their case before us, or have it pleaded for them on the stage; and we who watch observe that the dimensions of the situation, and hence also of the argument, begin to enlarge beyond personal horizons. The situation grows beyond the control of the antagonists, and tragic form and force take over.

Antigone's fierce loyalty to her father's memory and her brother's corpse becomes public and civic rebellion; Creon's self-confidence, gathering strength as it becomes the reasoned policy of an established government, is converted into impiety and cruelty. This is because the voice and vision of the tragic muse is also public, never wholly personal. She chooses for characters kings and queens, captains and princesses, because it has not occurred to her that purely private troubles are necessarily of any great interest. Her mode is historical; her men and

women are so placed on the social stage that their private
determinations are felt instinctively to touch the commonwealth; their private obsessions can be public mis-
takes. This is the voice of the chorus admonishing Antigone, and the voice of Teiresias warning Creon. This is
drama in the grand manner, according to which the proportion of what befalls seems to exceed the intentions
of the actors. They blow a tin trumpet, and lo! a whole
wall of assumed security collapses upon their heads.

Here is the ultimate rationalism of the Attic stage. It
demonstrates, over and over again, that the original decisions for weal and woe are human; they are framed
within the passions of men and women. These human
decisions can be caught up in combination with the
tyranny of circumstances and their effects multiplied.
And they multiply still more, to become suicides of
women, the despair and remorse of fathers, the self-
mutilation of an Oedipus; as their chemistry of destruction is reinforced by their mutual collisions and combina-
tions, as heroic will confronts its counter will and neither
is able to give way.

This tragic formula has an economy of its own,
strangely moving, but not altogether easy to accept.
Every platitude about Antigone's virtue and Haemon's
heroism and Creon's villainy will die on your lips. You
are invited to join in pity and fear, but beware lest your
moral judgments come too easy to you, and you defeat
in your minds the more complex intentions of the artist.

For the perennial fascination of the Greek tragic muse
lies in the fact that her accent is composite. She compre-

hends and understands the life of action and also the life of art, and offers a commentary upon both. The life without and the life within are both there, though it is characteristic of the high classic mood that the former should be dominant. In the end we are all public persons, and our private motives become public policies. Anouilh, in his version of the *Antigone,* saw this very well, and drew out some of the conclusions in a rather prolonged dialogue between Creon and Antigone: What are the procedures and responsibilities of power? Creon's edict denying the compassion of common burial does indeed deny our common nature. But if that were all, Creon would be a character not tragic but simply brutal and foolish. As it is, he is also the would-be statesman, anxious to conserve law and order, conscious of his responsibility to prevent rebellion and avert fresh civil wounds—and then, you see how his objectives are fatally defeated by the perverse faults of his own personality.

On the other hand, in the sphere of pure art, leaving public and political issues aside, how superbly satisfying are the patterns of this tragic form! Observe the delicate and intricate balances established between the two woman, Ismene and Antigone, and between the two men, Creon and his son, age versus youth. Observe the discreet but satisfying partition of the play between the two protagonists, Antigone and Creon. First the woman holds our attention, and then the man, while the woman retires to the cave of death; yet in her absence she still exercises remote control over the final crisis. Nor let us forget the exquisite symmetries of the antiphonal choruses that continually, by their lyric release, enlarge on the content of what is going on and make of these horrid events something at least acceptable, if not beautiful.

If Picasso's *Guernica* has a special relevance to this tragic form, it is surely for three corresponding reasons: It too celebrates a public affair and is itself a public affair conceived in a public medium as though it were a great fresco or temple pediment, oblong and symmetrical. It too is a portrayal of suffering and death; for what happened at Guernica was not a pretty story. And finally, in Picasso's painting there is still to be found the Greek chorus, the lady with the lamp, dismayed but not wholly overcome, shedding her dim light over the action—a classic face, a universal countenance. Is she not after all the ultimate voice of Greek rationalism and of Greek freedom of mind? All this that she surveys has to happen, but something or someone remains watching it, compassionate and striving to understand.

Can our culture find any present relevance here? Can it unite the turbulence of the life of action with the serenities of final comprehensive acceptance? We did manage this once, in an unexpected figure, who labored in a situation which was on the surface very untraditional. It is easy for us to associate the foundations of our republic with traditional and classic concepts of liberty under law. We can notice the classic decorum which infuses the prose of a Jefferson and observe the construction of a system of human rights and restraints which in spirit goes back to Pericles and Cicero. But it was a later statesman who at the crown of his career and in the tragic crisis of his country was able to formulate in American terms the Greek tragic experience, as he presided over a

35

country still torn by civil war, a house still divided between the rival claims of two protagonists:

Both parties deprecated war; but one of them would make war rather than let the nation survive, and the other would accept war rather than let it perish. And the war came. . . . Neither party expected for the war, the magnitude or duration which it has already obtained. Neither anticipated that the cause of the conflict might cease with, or even before, the conflict itself should cease. Each looked for an easier triumph, and a result less fundamental and astounding. Both read the same Bible, and pray to the same God, and each invokes His aid against the other. . . . The prayers of both could not be answered—those of neither have been answered fully. . . . Fondly do we hope, fervently do we pray, that this mighty scourge of war may soon pass away. Yet, if God wills that it continue until all the wealth piled by the bondsman's two hundred and fifty years of unrequited toil shall be sunk, and until every drop of blood drawn by the lash shall be paid by another drawn with the sword, as was said three thousand years ago, so still it must be said: "The judgments of the Lord are true and righteous altogether."

Certain phraseology here is from the Old Testament. But do not be misled. The spirit and substance never came out of the Old Testament. The touch of fatalism, the compassionate survey of both sides, the solemn criticism and commentary on human pride which gather up these two moral imperatives of North and South in a larger and more complicated pattern—here is the voice of the Greek chorus, as it spoke in Washington over ninety years ago. And as, I predict, it may some day speak again.

Etruscan Mirror, engraved:
ALEXANDER HELEN CHRYSEIS ACHILLES
IV-III cent. B.C., bronze

H. D. F. Kitto

THE QUESTION to which I shall try to give some sort of answer is this: Why is it that the plays of Sophocles refuse to die? Not only do they remain very much alive to the scholars who read them; not only does there appear a constant succession of translations; but they also compel the attention of the professional theatre to-day—not perhaps very often, but at least as often as, say, Racine and Corneille.

And not only this. There is also the fact that modern dramatists, from the seventeenth century on, have returned again and again to Sophocles, translating, imitating, adapting; the *Antigone* of Anouilh being the most conspicuous example. This, I think, can be called vitality, and it is natural to inquire what are the qualities of the Sophoclean drama which give it this vitality.

It is only for convenience that I limit myself to Sophocles. The subject of these essays is a wider one: the Vitality of the Classical Tradition; but I have preferred to concentrate on Sophocles partly from fear of getting lost in generalities; partly because Sophocles is eminently a classic of the classics, as typical of the Periclean Age as the Parthenon itself, so that what is said of Sophocles is likely to be true, *mutatis mutandis*, of the spirit of the classical tradition at large. Certainly, what I shall say about Sophocles I would also say, with some few modifications, of Aeschylus, and (perhaps with rather more modifications) of Euripides; and I suspect that much the same things would be said about the Greek visual arts by those capable of discussing them, which I am not.

But though I limit myself to Sophocles, there is another obvious extension of our inquiry which I must mention in passing. The *Antigone* of Anouilh reminds us that Anouilh also wrote a *Eurydice;* and that may remind us that Giraudoux has written *La Guerre de Troie n' aura pas Lieu;* and that may remind us that many other plays have been written in the present century which have not indeed taken a Greek play for their framework, like Anouilh's *Antigone*, but have taken a Greek myth as their foundation—as Eliot and O'Neill have both turned to the Orestes-legend. Shakespeare turned impartially to English or Scottish history, to Plutarch, to Italian *novelle;* only rarely to Classical myth. Racine used Roman, Greek, and Biblical history or myth. Present-day dramatists, when they *do* use myth, seem to prefer the Greek. Why?

Before we turn to Sophocles in particular, there is one more general point which might be mentioned; it is, I think, both interesting and important. More than once I have been asked, as an irreconcilable Hellenist, if I am not offended at the way in which Anouilh has taken over Sophocles' work wholesale and given it a completely new meaning. My reply has always been "No; why should I?" This is precisely what the Greek dramatists themselves were always doing—and that is one reason why their work is alive. The plays written by Aeschylus, Sophocles, and Euripides on the Orestes-myth are utterly different both in style and in meaning; and Euripides, just like Anouilh, introduces anachronisms not because he is careless but because he wants them. The irritation which a Classical pedant might feel at Anouilh could hardly be greater than the rage felt by Schlegel at Euripides' *Electra*. The fact that the French play is based on ideas which could not have occurred to a Greek makes it the more interesting that its author should have turned to a Greek play for his dramatic framework. The Greek dramatic form showed vitality when Milton used it for his *Samson*—no pious revival, like Matthew Arnold's tedious and frigid *Merope*, but new wine for which Milton chose an old bottle—and not with the disastrous result which occurred in the parable. Manifestly then, the old bottle has tough qualities. What are they?

The answer toward which I shall try to argue, in examining Sophocles' *Antigone,* is in two parts. The first is that his drama springs always, and directly, from certain deep apprehensions about some of the fundamental conditions of human existence; that is, in the language of the Greek poets, about the relations of man with the gods. They are not simply plays about exciting or tragic persons, though his persons are indeed exciting. It used to be the accepted view of Sophocles—it can be found in Jebb—that he was a great artist, supreme in the delineation of characters and the devising of plots, but nothing of a thinker; that in matters of religion, for example, he was content with an orthodox piety. This, I am convinced, is a grave error; and I think that it sprang from what will be the second part of my argument: that Sophocles is one of those creative artists in whom intellectual strength and imaginative power are not only perfectly matched but also completely fused; what he apprehends and what he creates are indistinguishable the one from the other.

I pick up an interesting article on Russian painters of today. I read that one of them has painted a picture of a luscious female, on a barge, in the company of a very fat pig which is playing a trumpet; that a Russian art-critic explained to the writer of the article what the significance was: it had to do with the submission of beauty to the bestial passions; that the painter himself, being present, told the writer—discreetly speaking in French —that he had in fact been trying to illustrate the delirium of an invalid. This may be art, but it is not Sophoclean art; in Sophocles there is no such gap between what the mind of the artist has apprehended and what his imagination has created. If, as I have suggested, what Sophocles apprehends in each play is some fundamental aspect of human existence, and if it is this which he realizes, sharply and clearly, in what his imagination creates, it seems to follow that the dramatic forms that he invents—whether characters or situations or plots— will have the qualities of basic simplicity and universality. They will have something in common with those basic elements of stage-design—the rostrum, the throne, the flight of steps—out of which the modern stage-designer can construct such telling effects.

Let us spend a few minutes contemplating the *Antigone*, in the hope that they will make these generalities clearer. I venture to ask a question which, in some quarters today, is considered a vulgar question to ask about a work of art: What is the play about? Ask this question about the picture of the lady with the trumpeteering pig, and the answer apparently is "Your guess is as good as mine." Ask it about the *Antigone*, and the answer apparently is "Your guess is not as good as mine"—or rather (since that is an immodest thing to say) "We don't *need* to guess; the meaning, and nothing else, is clearly expressed in the form."

What *is* the *Antigone* about? It is not in order to be eccentric that I will begin with the *end* of the play. My reason is that many of Sophocles' admirers—Mr. D. W. Lucas being the latest—think that Sophocles made a mess of it. They think this because they have not realized

how a great artist works, and how he is to be understood.
In the last hundred verses or so of the play Antigone's
name is not mentioned, and *her* body is not brought back
from the tomb, only Haemon's. There is a second body
presently, but it is Eurydice's. Mr. Lucas indicates that
his interest in the play is much attenuated when Antigone disappears from it. Somebody therefore has made
a mistake. I shall argue that it is not Sophocles; and that
if it is not Sophocles, important consequences follow.

Beginning then at the end, and (let us hope) being
willing to assume that Sophocles probably knew what
he was doing, we observe this: that we are looking at
Creon confronted by the bodies of his son and his wife—
that is, with the total ruin of his house. We may remember how he lectured Haemon about discipline and family
solidarity; his own family he has destroyed, and he says
now, more than once "It is my own fault, my own folly.
I have slain you, my son, and you, my wife." He has
also slain Antigone; but either Sophocles has forgotten
the fact—which seems unlikely—or he has judged that
this is not the important fact *at this moment*. It is with
Creon, with his folly, his misery, his remorse, that the
play ends. The last word is given to the chorus:

> Of Happiness, far the greatest part
> Is Wisdom, and Reverence towards the gods.
> Proud words of the arrogant man, in the end,
> Bring punishment, great as his pride was great,
> Till at last he is schooled in Wisdom.

Have we not heard this before? Yes; in the first ode,

when the chorus was thinking of the arrogant frenzy of one of the Argive champions, Capaneus, who was struck down by Zeus from the battlements:

> For the arrogant boast of the impious man
> Zeus hateth exceedingly . . .
> Ζεὺς γὰρ μεγάλης γλώσσης κομποὺς
> ὑπερεχθαίρει . . .

Μεγάλης γλώσσης κομπούς in Capaneus; μεγάλοι λόγοι in Creon: they bring μεγάλας πληγάς to each; great words, and great disaster.

This is where Sophocles chose to end his play—with all the weight thrown upon the folly of Creon and his ruin.

Working backward, passing over the Messenger's speech and the desperate appeal to Dionysus in the sixth ode, we come to the one character whom Anouilh did not want—Teiresias. Why did Sophocles want him? The first reason is obvious enough: it is Teiresias, with his authority, and his threat, who at last breaks the obstinacy of Creon—and incidentally convinces the chorus too; for up to this moment the chorus has believed that Antigone was wrong to defy the King. But Teiresias does much more than this. Neither Sophocles nor Shakespeare uses prophecy and divine action merely as a dramatic convenience. Teiresias begins by describing events which are contrary to the natural order: birds are screaming unnaturally and tearing each other; fat laid on a blazing altar—βωμοῖσι παμφλέκτοισι—will not catch fire. The cause is the unnatural things that Creon has done: he has

45

buried a living soul, and has refused burial to a dead body; therefore the upper gods and the nether gods are angry with him, and the Erinyes, their unerring ministers of vengeance, are lying in wait for him. And not only that: he has aroused the same wrath among men—in the cities of those men whose unburied bodies are sending pollution to their own hearths and altars. In self-defense, against such pollution, they are banding together against him. Creon has incurred the opposition both of gods and of men.

When Teiresias tells us at such length about birds who are fighting and fat which will not burn, it is reasonable to think for a moment about the opening of *Oedipus Rex*, where the same kind of symbolism is used. Innocently, Oedipus has greatly offended against two of Nature's fundamental laws, against two of humanity's deepest instincts: he has killed his father and married his mother. The result is similar: since these acts go unpunished, because unknown, Nature at last rises in revolt: there is a plague—and the form which the plague takes is full of meaning, for it is sterility: crops, animals, the human kind, are all barren. It is not unreasonable to think also of *Hamlet*—not that Shakespeare imitated Sophocles, but that the great religious tragic poets have a *lingua franca*: a brother has murdered a brother and corrupted his wife; therefore

> the sepulchre
> Wherein we saw thee quietly inurn'd
> Hath oped his ponderous and marble jaws

to send the Ghost forth, making night hideous. The gods will not for long endure such crimes; Nature rises in rebellion against things done contrary to Nature. Such things too Creon has done.

What do the gods do? Is there an angry, black-robed Erinys who descends upon Creon? No; we have seen what Creon suffers. Sophocles makes it quite clear why he suffers, and that it comes about in a perfectly natural way. On a superficial view the gods do nothing—but let us try not to be superficial. We must go further back in the play, to the scene between Creon and his son.

Haemon came in hoping to reason with Creon, doing his best to be conciliatory. Public opinion, as he knows, is with him. Creon, for all his talk of discipline and unity within family and city, is isolating himself from Thebes, from humanity, above all from his loyal son; and it is cruelly suitable that his punishment comes not in his own death but in that of his son and of his twice-bereaved wife. Creon rejects Haemon's plea for Antigone—not with sympathy and understanding, but brutally and coarsely, as he has already spoken coarsely to Ismene of Haemon's love. This coarse and harsh indifference is the whole point; it drives Haemon to the pitch where he can endure it no longer.

At this point Sophocles does a most important thing: he makes the chorus reflect on the power of Love—Eros, Aphrodite; a power supreme among gods, men, animals; a power with which it is dangerous to trifle. When the chorus says "Love perverts the mind even of the upright man" it is thinking of Haemon's unfilial conduct—not the only time in the play that the chorus is made to say the significant thing, but with reference to the wrong person. But we, the audience, being warned that Aphrodite is powerful, not to be trifled with—what do *we* think when we hear of Haemon's frenzied attack on his father at the tomb, and of his suicide? What *can* we think —if we are in imaginative contact with the religion of the Greek dramatists—but that in the lover's rage we see Aphrodite at work? Creon imagined that Haemon's deep love for Antigone was something that he could sweep aside: "There are women enough; let him marry somebody else." Creon was wrong; Aphrodite does not recognize a King's decree.

It was not true, then, that the gods and their Erinys do nothing in their anger against Creon; Aphrodite, for one, does a great deal. Nor do men do nothing. Creon's late repentance does indeed forestall the threatened march of the armies; but Creon's act drives the impetuous Antigone to suicide, and the rest follows naturally. This is the way in which the Erinys of the gods does her work.

I am not the first to observe that Sophocles, unlike Shakespeare in *Romeo and Juliet,* unlike Anouilh in *Antigone,* unlike any modern dramatist whom one could name or imagine, writes no scene in which his tragic lovers meet. The conclusion has been drawn that Sophocles, being an Athenian, had no interest in romantic love—a complete misconception. What does not interest him, as a tragic dramatist, is the exploitation or contemplation of romantic love on the personal level. The love which these two young people bear for each other, as I

48

hope I have shown, is a most important part of the theme; it is the pivot on which Creon's tragedy turns. To bring them together on the stage might have been an interesting thing to do; it was not a *necessary* thing, and therefore Sophocles will not do it. Haemon's love for Antigone becomes, in the play, one of those elemental forces in human life which Creon, in his blindness, thinks he can disregard and sweep aside.

But if this is true, what is the connection, if any, between the love-theme and Antigone's heroic determination to bury her brother? The connection is close and direct. To see what it is we must go from the Haemon-scene, in our disorderly examination of the play, both backward and forward, because in both directions we find Antigone the focus of our attention. Let us go forward first.

Immediately after that short ode about Love, Antigone is led in, guarded. There follows the long lyrical dialogue between her and the chorus—ten minutes of singing—and in the theatre ten minutes are a long time. Creon remains on stage, visible, motionless. The fact is both clear and important. Antigone, almost insulted by the frigid consolations which are all that this politically-minded chorus can offer, sings her life away in what is surely one of the most poignant scenes in drama. Creon is there, and it means nothing to him. It means so little that he breaks in at last with the order that this noise shall stop at once.

This was important to Sophocles. That is the reason why he keeps Creon on stage. The point is that his behavior here exactly parallels his behavior toward Haemon: each time he is utterly indifferent to a claim of simple humanity which, to a normal man, would be overwhelming. Another man might indeed think that in this case his duty was clear, repugnant though it might be; such a man in fact is the Creon of Anouilh. But the Creon of Sophocles does not even feel the repugnance; the appeals to humanity made by Ismene, by Haemon, and by Antigone in her lyrics, only make him angry. The agony that awaits Antigone, the despair of his son, are to him things that do not matter. He is to discover that they do.

When we go backward, to the first part of the play, we find the same thing. Here it is important to be clear on two points: one is the nature of the religious duty which Antigone feels; the other is the nature of the fate from which she saves Polyneices. Let us take the second first.

In his *Antigone,* Anouilh writes vividly about the uneasy ghost of Polyneices flitting about in the underworld: where did he get the idea from? Not from Sophocles; he got it from the commentators on Sophocles. In Sophocles there is not a single word about the fate of Polyneices' soul; it is the learned commentators who have brought this into the play, and by bringing this in they have inevitably pushed something else out. What they have pushed out is that on which Sophocles lays all his emphasis: three times reference is made to the body that shall not be buried, and each time what is emphasized is the sheer physical horror—one which we ourselves can feel no less than the Greeks—of the devouring of a human body by animals.

Then what about Antigone's "religious duty," since the

mystical connotation is due to the commentators, not to Sophocles?

In a Greek context, the word "religion" is treacherous. How difficult it is for us to understand that a play like *Lysistrata* was a perfectly natural part of a "religious" festival! It is a Roman word by origin, and by constant association it has become a Christian word, with strong ecclesiastical overtones. Let us avoid it therefore, and use Antigone's own language. She is doing what the gods demand.

In the *Electra,* Orestes and Electra were doing this too when they killed their mother—a fact which is a grave embarrassment so long as we equal piety and holiness with "religion"; for where is the holiness in killing your mother? But all becomes clear when we realize what the Greek gods prefigured to the Greeks: *quod semper, quod ubique,* the basic laws or forces that are interwoven with human affairs. Clytemnestra and Aegisthus assassinated a King, usurped his crown and his estate, and are living in adultery; such crimes will naturally generate a violent recoil. It is the inevitable result; it is a law of the gods. Similarly it is instinctive in mankind—we today can call it a sacred instinct if we like— to treat with respect the dead body of a fellow human being. It is what the gods demand. Antigone cannot and will not endure that her own brother's body shall be mangled by animals. How can she prevent this? Never mind; she *does* prevent it. Can a light covering of dust keep hungry animals from a rich store of meat? Have you ever seen a dog rummaging through a garbage pail for a bone? What nonsense this is! Never mind; her dust *does* keep away the animals—until the guards remove it; the Watchman tells us so—and the chorus-leader gives us the clue:

Do we not see in this the hand of God?

It is not always wise to be prosaic over poetry. In resisting this unnatural and revolting outrage Antigone is working with the gods, and the gods with her. This is the first time in the play that Creon vainly pits himself against the gods, against something that is fundamental to human existence. The second time is when he presumes to ignore the power of Aphrodite. This is the connection between the love-theme and Antigone's passionate, instinctive resistance to Creon. For we should observe how many motives are given to Antigone: what we call the "religious" motive, and family loyalty, and indignation that Creon, an outsider, should presume to intervene in a sacred family rite. On her part it is rebellion total and instinctive. This is the way in which the gods work.

For these deep human instincts are one of the regions in which the Greek gods are at home. As Poseidon moves in the sea and Zeus in the lightning; as mountains and rivers and forests are full of gods; so are these sacred instincts divine, like the reverence a man has for his parents, the loyalty that he bears toward his kin or his city, the forbearance he shows, or should show, toward the defenseless, the instinctive respect that he feels toward a dead body, the love that a man and a woman share. It is against things like this that Creon offends, repeatedly, and they are avenged on him, in the natural course. He disregards laws that are written in no statute-book, but are laws of nature, of humanity, of the gods. He angers the gods, and they strike; the consequences of his own folly recoil on him. The provocation was great; the crime of Polyneices was intolerable. So, in another play, was the attempted crime of Ajax; there too the commanders whom he had tried to murder deny burial to his body. But Sophocles says the same thing there as here: burial of a body is a tribute of respect which humanity owes to itself. The claims of simple humanity are paramount, and the natural human sanctities—love, loyalty, pity—are things that you flout at your peril.

This has been a very brief examination of the play. Our point of departure was the assertion that Sophocles' drama is always concerned with something fundamental to human existence, and that what the poet apprehends on this level is completely transmuted into dramatic terms. I hope that so much at least has been made to appear acceptable—that the play concerns something even more fundamental than a conflict between State law and private conscience; and that incidentally, when we see this, we also see how well-designed the play is. No longer need our interest evaporate when Antigone leaves the stage.

This is the point at which to answer a possible objection, which, optimistically, I will put like this: "You have propounded an interpretation which, for the sake of argument, I will accept. I will admit too that we mod-

erns, not being fifth-century Greeks, may have to recon-
struct, by careful analysis of plays, religious ideas which
were instinctive in Sophocles' audience. But are we really
to suppose that the ordinary Athenian saw as much as
this in the play? And if not, what would it mean to *him?*"

My answer would be that the transmutation of
thought into drama is so complete that the plays *live* at
any level, and have a significance at any level. Let us
take the Teiresias scene as a example. At the most un-
sophisticated level it might be felt, and reported, after
this fashion:

> All of a sudden, out of the blue, an old man comes in
> —blind, a prophet. Fair made me sit up! The King
> seems frightened. The old man tells him what he
> knows, from the birds and a sacrifice that wouldn't
> burn. He says the King is wrong about not burying
> the body, and he'd better give way. The King flies into
> a rage; says somebody has been bribing the prophet.
> "Oh," says he, "that's what you think, is it? Then listen
> to me"; and he tells him that he has been downright
> wicked, not burying the one body and burying the girl
> alive; and that the gods are angry, and that somebody
> of his own family is going to die because of it. Then he
> goes out, and the King crumples up. And by God it all
> comes true!

This may be very crude, and it misses a lot, but even
so it is impressive and it is significant. It lives.

There is the more sophisticated level already referred
to, that of Mr. Lucas and those who think like him. Much
of the real excitement of the play is perceived, and the
important political theme; the conflict between Creon

and Antigone is appreciated, though not the deeper conflict which really unifies the play, namely that between
Creon and the gods. On this level the play is very much
alive, even though the last scenes provoke a yawn. Contrast this with certain serious plays of the present day
which I could mention but do not: they have, no doubt,
important content, but my modest experience of them
is that unless you see what the dramatist is getting at
(which I rarely do), they are dull. At my level they
hardly live at all. Either the philosophic content is such
as can hardly be transmuted into drama, or the dramatist's creative imagination is not strong enough for the
job.

The position which we have now reached is that the
classical Greek drama, and classical Greek art in general,
deals with some of those simple profundities which concern us all, simply as members of the human race; they
are not individual or local or temporary matters. Compare Aeschylus and Sophocles with Theocritus or Henry
James. Theocritus was, I think, a poet of genius; a lovely
singer—but by comparison he sings rather small. James
will make an elaborate, delicate and entirely absorbing
study of, say, an honest American mistrustfully regarding the complexities of aristocratic Paris. It is no dispar-
agement of James to say that here is material which is
temporal and local, not universal.

But does all this mean more than that Sophocles was
a tragic poet, and said the kind of thing that tragic poets
normally do? No. Yet obviously there *is* more. Obviously
there is something that distinguishes the Greek from

later tragic poets, if only that their dramatic form is so different. What started us off was the fact that a modern dramatist can take over a Greek play wholesale and use it afresh; how surprising it would be if he should have done this with *Hamlet* or *Othello!* There is clearly something more than profundity, universality, and vividness.

The answer may lie—or part of it—in the unusual concentration that one always finds in classical Greek art; this may be an important cause, too, of its continuing vitality. I will illustrate this, if I can, by asking you to consider for a moment another of Sophocles' plays, the *Electra*. Here we have Sophocles' version of the return of Orestes, and the vengeance which he and Electra exact from Agamemnon's murderers. The first scene, some hundred verses, is played by Orestes, the silent Pylades, and Orestes' old slave. When they go out, Electra comes on; and she remains on the stage, always the center of interest, always acting hard, until the end of the play, except for an interval of about a quarter of a minute. It is a dramatic role like no other that I know; not only is it a long one, but also it covers the whole range of human emotion, from pure love to terrible hatred, from utter despair to exultation. She begins on a low pitch of lamentation for her father. When the Chorus offers sympathy and advice she speaks bitterly of the murder, resentfully of Orestes' long delay. Then comes a long speech, and a most vivid one, describing the hatefulness of her daily life in the palace with the two assassins and usurpers. Then, when she hears that Clytemnestra has had a bad dream that seems to foreshadow vengeance, she hails it excitedly as a sign that the tide may at last be turning. Next comes the violent quarrel between mother and daughter; after which Clytemnestra, frightened by the dream, sacrifices to Apollo and prays for his protection against the threatened vengeance. She has her answer: the old slave enters, with the false tale of Orestes' death. Clytemnestra rejoices; Electra is shattered; everything that she has been living for lies in ruins. But she recovers her nerve, and presently is offering her sister, vainly, her chance of winning glory: the two of them will themselves kill Aegisthus. Then another swift change, for Orestes and Pylades enter, in the guise of strangers bringing home Orestes' ashes. This calls forth from Electra a most moving lament for the brother whom she loved and nurtured and saved as a baby. Orestes declares himself, and the mood of grief and despair is followed by one of ecstatic joy. Then comes the killing of Clytemnestra and Aegisthus. Electra is kept on the stage, in order that we may see how implacable is her hatred of them. When Aegisthus would parley with Orestes, Electra cries:

> No! no long speech from him! Kill him at once,
> Give him the burial that he deserves:
> Animals shall eat him!

We know what Sophocles thought about not burying the dead; the reappearance of the symbol here shows the awful extent of Electra's hatred.

Obviously, here is concentration indeed; one theme and one character dominate it entirely.

But when I spoke of "concentration" I meant more than this. My rapid summary of the play would give the impression that it was a vivid and elaborate study of a heroic character as it is affected by tragic circumstances, warped by oppression and hatred. The play certainly is this—but it is much more too; for in my summary I carefully left out the fact that Sophocles has interwoven with all this—as in the *Antigone*—the constant presence of the gods; not only of Apollo, but of Zeus too, and his daughter Dikê, and of the Erinyes, and of the gods of the underworld. Jebb explained that Sophocles, being just an artist, interested only in character, situation and plot, thought the moral implications of the story none of his business. Sheppard, on the other hand, avoids the difficulty by asserting that Orestes got it all wrong: Apollo was not in favor of the matricide. But these are difficulties of our own making. Here, as elsewhere, the gods may represent not what ought to be, but what *is*— *quod semper, quod ubique.* Sin has been committed— murder, adultery, usurpation. These are offences against the gods, against Dikê, against Nature; and, as we have seen, such offences are likely, in the normal course of things, to generate their own recoil. That is what Sophocles displays here. Two of Agamemnon's children are not such as to acquiesce in the crime. Orestes, being a man of honor, is determined, naturally, to avenge his father and to recover his throne and his patrimony. Electra is of the same temper and mind; and Sophocles so treats her, and the circumstances of her life, that we see how every detail impels her more and more to dedicate herself to vengeance. Her bitter hatred of the murderers, her awful cry "Throw him to the dogs!" are not held up to us as admirable, nor is the deed of vengeance, even though the gods are concerned in it all. They are held up as the natural consequence of the original offence. That was ugly; why should its recoil be pretty?

I shall take two of the speeches, as I think they will show us how completely Sophocles transmuted his thought into drama. Here is Electra's first speech to the Chorus:

> What woman would not cry to Heaven, if she
> Had any trace of spirit, when she saw
> Her father suffering outrage, such as I
> Must look on every day—and every night?
> And it does not decrease, but always grows
> More insolent. There is my mother: she—
> My mother!—has become my bitterest enemy;
> And then, I have to share my house with those
> Who murdered my own father; I am ruled
> By them, and what I get—what I must do
> Without—depends on them. What happy days,
> Think you, mine are, when I must see Aegisthus
> Sitting upon my father's throne, wearing
> My father's robes, and pouring his libations
> Beside the hearth-stone where they murdered *him*?
> And I must look upon the crowning outrage:
> The murderer lying in my father's bed
> With my abandoned mother—if I must
> Call her a mother who dares sleep with him!
> She is so brazen that she lives with that
> Defiler; vengeance from the gods is not
> A thought that frightens *her*! As if exulting

In what she did, she noted carefully
The day on which she treacherously killed
My father, and each month, when that day comes,
She holds high festival, and sacrifices
Sheep to the Gods her Saviours.—I look on
In misery, and weep with breaking heart.
This cruel mockery, her *Festival
Of Agamemnon*, is to me a day
Of bitter grief—and I must grieve alone.
And then, I cannot even weep in peace:
This noble lady bids me stop, reviles
Me bitterly: "You god-forsaken creature!
You hateful thing! are you the only one
Who ever lost a father? Has none but you
Ever worn black? A curse upon you! May
The gods of Hades give you ample cause
To weep for evermore!" So she reviles me.
But when she hears from someone that Orestes
May come, she flies into a frenzied rage,
Stands over me and screams: "It's you I have
To thank for this, my girl! This is *your* work!
You stole Orestes from my hands, and sent
Him secretly away. But, let me tell you,
I'll make you pay for this as you deserve."
So, like a dog, she yelps, encouraged by
That milksop coward, that abomination,
That warrior who shelters behind women.
    My cry is for Orestes and his coming,
To put an end to this. Oh, I am sick
At heart for waiting. He is holding back,
And his delay has broken all my hopes.

There is no need to make phrases about the terrific
impact which this makes; of the swift and vivid way in

which it sets the character of Electra before us, and pre-
pares us for all that is to come. Let us instead think of
something else, for the speech does more than draw a
portrait. If the underlying conception is that crime gen-
erates its own recoil, that the gods and Dikê too are
active in this affair, then the speech shows *how* Dikê and
the gods work; we are made to feel how the monstrous
situation produced by the crime so works on Electra that
she can do no other but resent it and resist it. Dramatic
power and philosophic thought are "of imagination all
compact." There is no need for the dramatist to make
generalized philosophic statement about the underlying
thought; all that is said directly through the drama.

The other speech is the one which Electra makes as
she holds the urn which contains, as she supposes,
Orestes' ashes. This too could be regarded as no more
than an extension of character-drawing: we have seen
how she can hate; now we are to see how she could love.
True; but this is incidental. There is much more; and I
think this would be obvious to Greek audience which
had the Greek way of thinking about the Greek gods.

> Orestes! my Orestes! You have come
> To this! The hopes with which I sent you forth
> Are come to this! How radiant you were!
> And now I hold you—so; a little dust.
> Oh, would to God that I had died myself,
> And had not snatched *you* from the edge of death
> To have you sent into a foreign land!
> They would have killed you, but you would have shared
> Your father's death and burial; not been killed

Far from your home, an exile, pitiably,
Alone, without your sister. Not for you,
The last, sad tribute of a sister's hand!
Some stranger washed your wounds, and laid your body
On the devouring fire; the charity
Of strangers brings you home—so light a burden,
And in so small a vessel!
                          O my brother,
What love and tenderness I spent on you!
For you were my child rather than your mother's;
I was your nurse, or you would not have had
A nurse. I was the one you always called
Your *sister*—and it has come to nothing.
One single day has made it all in vain
And, like a blast of wind, has swept it all
To ruin. You are dead; my father too
Lies in his grave. Your death is death to me,
Joy to our enemies. Our mother—if
She is a mother—dances in delight;
When you had sent me many a secret message
That you would come and be revenged on her.
But no; a cruel fate has ruined you
And ruined me, and brought it all to nothing.
The brother that I loved is gone, and in
His place are ashes, and an empty shadow.
O pity! Pity, grief and sorrow!
How cruel, cruel is your homecoming,
My dearest brother. I can live no longer.
O take me with you! You are nothing; I
Am nothing, now. Let me henceforward be
A shade among the shades, with you. We lived
As one; so now in death let us be one,
And share a common grave, as while you lived
We shared a common life. O let me die,
For death alone can put an end to grief.

Now, more than once in the play the existence and power of the gods—that is to say, the existence of an ordered and not a chaotic universe—has been equated with the return and the triumph of Orestes. The Chorus has said: "Zeus sees and rules all things; Orestes will some day return with the kindly escort of Zeus; wickedness will not triumph for ever; Dikê will come and assert her might." But the burden of Electra's speech is that all her love, devotion, courage, have come to nothing; all was in vain. Orestes is dead, and the murderers are laughing. Have the gods failed? Is life without meaning? Is death the only remedy? The answer to these despairing questions is on the stage, for us to see: Orestes is alive!

Once more, the drama lives at any level. If we miss the philosophic implications and see only the personal ones, nevertheless these are most moving. But one reason why the play as a whole is so impressive, so concentrated, so vital, is that on the personal level it is the reverse of diffuse; it is not discursive or merely descriptive; no aspects of character or situation are introduced merely because they are possible and interesting—just as, in the *Antigone*, there was no tragic love-scene for Antigone and Haemon. We have looked at only two speeches, but wherever we looked we should find the same direct and necessary relation between the drama and the thought.

This it is that I meant when I spoke of "concentration." Greek tragic drama is not unique in being profound, nor in being strong, nor in being exciting. It is unique in this high degree of concentration. It is markedly intellectual;

but it is just as strong imaginatively. Here at least intellectualism does not connote abstraction, aloofness, aridity—though traces of this do begin to show themselves now and then in the work of Euripides. But in general the Greek tragic poets persuade us of this: that they have contemplated the human scene with all the sympathetic awareness of which the creative artist is capable; that as philosophic thinkers they have thought their way through this and have reached some underlying and unifying principle—much as Thales, Anaximander and the rest did with the physical universe; and that finally, as artists again, they have recreated this underlying truth entirely in terms of human action and suffering; so that the play becomes not a slice taken from life, but something more like a vertical section of life, so taken as to reveal something of its foundations.

Is not this perhaps the reason why the dramatic forms which they invented have retained their vitality and validity—much as the architectural forms which they invented have done? I have mentioned *Hamlet* and *Othello*. Here we have profundity indeed and dramatic power; but why is it that we cannot imagine a dramatist taking them over and reworking them, as Anouilh has done with the *Antigone*? I would suggest at least a partial answer. One of the dramatist's problems is to make the play both a vivid particular story—what so-and-so did and suffered—and one which reveals a universal truth. The play must live on both levels. Now, Shakespeare no doubt has many ways of universalizing his particulars, but certainly one of them is what might be called the method of extension; for example, a by-plot will repeat the moral pattern of the main plot, and by repeating it will reinforce and universalize it. Consider this idea of extension with reference to *Hamlet*. You may agree that part at least of the burden of the play is the corrupting power of evil. See then how amply the idea of evil is presented. Not only does Claudius commit one crime after another; he is also a drunkard, and his physical appearance is mean—"Hyperion to a satyr." More than this: there is also his chief adviser Polonius, who has not only a crooked mind—and crooked speech too—and a dirty mind (for think how he speaks to Ophelia about Hamlet's love); but he is also one who can give high-sounding advice to his son, and then send a servant to Paris to spy on him, with suggestive innuendo. See too how amply the poison spreads. Both metaphorically and literally it abounds in the play, and the corruption poisons Gertrude, and Hamlet's mind, and betrays the honest Laertes into black treachery. It leads, directly or indirectly, to the total destruction of two houses, those of King Hamlet and of Polonius, and incidentally engulfs Rosencrantz and Guildenstern too.

Such extension, I suggest, gives the play great amplitude and richness, as well as its universality; with the result that *Hamlet* and *Othello* remain, splendidly and forever, *Hamlet* and *Othello*, far too complex and specific to serve the needs of an Anouilh. But Greek drama does not use the method of extension. Its way of universalizing the particular action is to interweave with it divine activity, the activity of law. Hence: concentration, not extension. Some permanent aspect of human experience is transmuted into a dramatic situation and dramatic persons with such concentration that the very form of it seems instinct with meaning, and can be used again and again.

And may not this be true of certain of the Greek myths? A myth like that of Orpheus and Eurydice, or of Prometheus and Zeus, or of Helen of Troy, seems instinct with meaning as the myth of Jack the Giant-killer is not; they are like those simple and potentially significant geometrical forms—steps, thrones, and the like—which the stage-designer can use over and over again for quite different purposes. Not that the myth in itself has any particular meaning—though it probably had to him who first framed it—but that it seems to be the last distillation of some profound aspect of human thought or experience, capable of being used again and again because human experience, at this deep level, does not change.

A final word on the vitality of the Classical tradition so far as Greek drama is concerned. The literary arts, especially perhaps drama, are in a different position from the visual arts; they are more vulnerable, in at least two ways. The obvious one is that unless we know their language, they must be translated for us, and the translator may be dull, or misguided, or an exhibitionist. It is not necessary to translate the Parthenon into concrete; it can speak to us directly. But in order to miss the vitality of Greek drama it is not even necessary to be ignorant of Greek (a handicap which need not be paralyzing): one need merely be interested not in drama but in something else, and use the plays as evidence for that something else. Treat the plays like this and they die on our hands —though the scholar who does it will usually not notice the difference. In our own times they have been used as an adjunct to anthropology; they have been dragged screaming to an altar and sacrificed to a theory of Dionysiac ritual sequence. A more recent fashion is to use them as evidence for the primitivism and darkness of thought in which today we take such delight and duly find in the drama of the fifth century—neglecting, naturally, all that is really dramatic in it. From such follies the Parthenon is safe. We look at it and are thrilled, or we study it in minute detail and are even more thrilled. We do not obscure it with a "background" of our own scholarly devising, and neglect, or explain away those parts of it which do not suit us. So should it be also with the plays. If we approach them as works of art, they will speak to us; if we treat them as documents to be used for other ends, they turn their backs on us and leave us to our own vain imaginings.

Votive Figurine, Iberic
ca. 500 B.C., bronze

FIGURE 19.

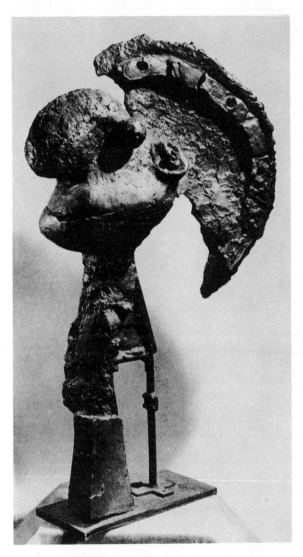

Picasso, *Head with Helmet*, 1933, bronze

Otto J. Brendel

THE NATURE OF THE PROBLEM

A QUOTATION from a recent book on the intellectual
condition of modern man will best introduce the
theme of this paper:

When the sensibility of an age can accommodate the alien
"inhuman" forms of primitive art side by side with the
classic "human" figures of Greece or the Renaissance, it
should be obvious that the attitude toward man that we call
classical humanism—which is the intellectual expression of
the spirit that informs the classical canon of Western art—

has also gone by the boards. This is an historical fact the most immediate evidence of which is the whole body of modern art itself.[1]

There is a ring of finality about these sentences which cannot fail to arrest the reader ("It should be obvious that . . . . This is an historical fact . . . ."). We feel confronted, not so much with a special observation or personal conclusion for which the responsibility lies with the author alone, as with a summary of a situation commonly acknowledged and easily verified by everyone and hence in need of no further discussion. Accordingly we accept this statement as an expression of beliefs typical rather than unique, representing currently widespread opinions on the matter of modern art, in particular of "modernism" as opposed to "classicism" in our time. At precisely this point we perceive the problem which interests us, and with which the following essay will deal. For in human affairs any opinion so widely shared is also apt to confirm, indeed to promote, the conditions it professes to recognize. Such an opinion, in brief, is more often than not an indication of intent as well as an expression of fact, likely therefore to conceal as much as it reveals. It invites the critical question: how do these matters really stand?

From the premise that modern taste evidently tolerates both "inhuman" primitive and classical "human" forms, it does not at once follow that "classical humanism . . . has also gone by the boards." Rather we are forced to conclude that in the world of today no kind of humanism, either the classical or any other, has an exclusive claim on expressing to our satisfaction our knowledge of, and our demands upon, the human status. This is indeed correct; nor is the case unusual. Over the centuries classical humanism has commonly had to compete with other rival and even opposing, philosophies, both religious-Christian, and secular-naturalistic. For all that, it did not become extinct; nor is it extinct today. The question must at least be left open as to what share, if any, classical humanism holds in the shaping of modern thought. We may have to ask ourselves whether we are prepared to recognize manifestations of that humanism if and when we meet them in a modern, unconventional context. For classical humanism cannot be spoken of as a set system of thought, as if it were a creed with a well-defined dogma. It is merely an interpretation of extant testimonies from the antiquity now labeled "classical," and perhaps a protestation of their undiminished validity and applicability to the human condition in general. At any rate, the interpretation of classical content, as well as its selection, is on every level a posthumous reaction. It is not necessarily a true exploration of ancient thought. The latter remark certainly applies to the very concept of the classical; the Greeks did not think of themselves as "classical." From the outset we may expect that the trends expressed in these belated interpretations change with the times, taking their directions from the special interests of the succeeding generations. For this reason we must seriously consider the possibility that, if such trends operate in our contemporary society at all, they will not always be readily spotted in their modern disguises. The chance that such is indeed the case is especially strong in modern art, where the stress is on a thorough transformation and radical recasting of all conventional concepts and modes of presentation. More than any other, this art has set out to change the familiar into forms of strangeness and, vice versa, to demonstrate the extraordinary in terms of the seemingly familiar.

THE ACADEMIC TRADITION: CREATION AND IMITATION

ONE facet of classicism that specifically concerns the visual arts is the academic tradition. I shall use this term to refer to the theories and practices characteristic of the professional academies engaged in the encouragement of the arts, in the training of young artists, and frequently, in the sustenance of an official level of taste. Academic trends in this sense had begun to form among artists and connoisseurs in the late sixteenth century but could exert a full impact only after they became confirmed by official institutions, such as the French and the British royal academies of art. On the whole, the academic tradition must be held a product of the seventeenth century, especially concomitant with the more pro-classical tendencies of the Baroque. The movement was definitely post-Renaissance, and in many ways epigonous from the start.

There is at present no single study of the academic

tradition to which we can refer, but the outcome of such a study may be anticipated to an extent.[2]

The academic doctrine, to call it so, was principally an educational theory. Its aim was to insure the creation and continuance of a classical style or, at least, of a grand manner of art. To further this purpose it recommended a selection of masterpieces to serve as models to the artist, and of subjects worthy of his efforts. From the seventeenth century on, the controversies in the French academy about art turned very much on subject matter, contrasting the noble themes of history, religion, and mythology to the lowly, generally disrespected, portrayals of such ordinary matters as landscapes, peasants, or still-lifes. By now this discussion has more or less died down. But it explains, for instance, why in Paris during most of the nineteenth century the objections to modern art that were publicly aired after each annual *Salon* were still concerned primarily, and most heatedly, with subjects held to be too realistic to suit the dignity of art.

More interesting and of more immediate importance for the present are some problems that resulted from the other aspect of the academic tradition, the recommended models. The list included from the beginning a core of famous antiques, mostly statues from Roman collections, selected by consensus of the connoisseurs and publicized by all available means. This selection of exemplars proved to be the most lasting as well as the most tangible item in the academic program. It was indeed the belief in these exemplars, their wide distribution by graphic reproduction or plaster casts, and the constant faithful study of the latter which established the academic tradition, reinforcing an otherwise vaguely classicistic taste with the authority of the schools and the firmness of a continuous practice. By the seventeenth century the selection was already quite standarized, the top place being held by such undisputed masterpieces as the Laocoön group, the Belvedere Torso, or the Medici Venus. The eighteenth century added little to the list; in the early nineteenth century, the list was augmented by a small number of Greek originals which became rapidly popular, such as the Parthenon sculptures and the Venus of Milo. Yet by and large the lists were closed, or nearly so. Meanwhile, however, the plaster casts of the accepted masterpieces continued to be used in the schools and the academies of art as a means of instruction; they had become a professional emblem of the artist's studio. It is also worth noting that in this limited usage, at least, classicism acquired a definite and definable meaning: it meant adherence to the recommended models.[3]

Obviously this state of affairs exhibits rather special features. The narrowness of the selection may well surprise us; so may its constancy. The number of masterpieces thus picked as exemplary was small indeed compared to the mass of ancient art preserved and already known by the seventeenth century. Nor did the vast increase of materials contributed by the discoveries and excavations of scholars since the late nineteenth century leave much impress on the tradition carried on in the academies of art. By then this tradition had long become saturated. It had no place left for Greek archaic art or the sculptures from Olympia, for example. Its function was no longer truly selective. Rather it had turned into a program of standardization, operating in the restricted use of recommended models and in the very realm of judgment as well, which determined what was and what was not deemed classical. In the definition of the schools whose needs were practical, whose interests critical, and whose tastes conservative, "classical" had become synonymous with "exemplary"; not all ancient art qualified.

It is necessary to emphasize the contrast between this academic restrictiveness and the freedom displayed by the Renaissance artists in their encounters with ancient art. The Renaissance attitude appears definitely pre-academic in any such comparison. I doubt if the role played by the ancient prototypes in the art of the fifteenth century and even in the so-called high Renaissance has yet been sufficiently made clear. Nor can this be easily accomplished, for the Renaissance approach to classical art was so much less dogmatic, less prejudiced, and more adventurous than the academic. The catalogue of ancient models used by Renaissance artists, at one time and another, is surprisingly large. It includes many works of the minor arts on a small scale, such as coins and engraved gems, a great deal of relief work such as Roman sarcophagi, and much that we would judge to be of mediocre quality.[4] In brief, the Renaissance taste in ancient monuments appears to have been considerably more catholic and less critically exclusive than that of the later academies.

The liberties taken by the artists of the Renaissance in transmuting their models were commensurably great. Renaissance painting and sculpture are permeated by reminiscences of ancient art, but often these citations are so freely rendered and transformed, so remote from their original settings and contexts, that the unsuspecting eye is hardly aware of them. It means little, therefore, to spot an ancient prototype in a Renaissance work. The really interesting problems appear when we begin to ask why a certain prototype was chosen at all, and why it was used in the particular way in which we happen to notice it. There is no uniform answer to these questions. The most personal question, what precisely pleased an artist about a foreign form which he chose to appropriate, remains always open, and the answers must vary according to the case at hand and the temperaments of the artists concerned. Titian selected his ancient models for purposes which differed widely from those of, say, Michelangelo. Also, reasons may be sought in any one of several, different directions. An artist's particular choice may have been prompted by his preferences for formal styling, or his interest in expressive gesture, or simply his vivid sensation of the greater power contained in an ancient image. It would be quite independent of the size and the manner of execution of the monument in which such an image came to his attention. In each case the choice testifies to the freshness and poignancy of a real discovery. This element of the personal and unexpected was all too often lost when artistic classicism moved into its academic phase.

For illustration one instance must here suffice, out of the available multitude. About 1500 Leonardo drew a *Kneeling Leda* (fig. 1) who bears a remarkable resemblance to a once famous Greek statue, the *Crouching Venus,* probably a work of the Hellenistic sculptor, Doidalsas (fig. 2). That is to say, Leonardo rendered the posture of kneeling in a manner decidedly similar to that of the ancient statue but changed completely the upper part, including the arms and head. It is nevertheless probable that the *Leda* was actually drawn with a knowledge of the ancient Venus of which several copies are still extant. For in a later work of Leonardo, the very unusual painting of St. John (fig. 3), reminiscences of the same composition come again to the fore. Only this time the similarities relate to the upper part, the head and the arms, of the *Crouching Venus.* Thus far we can follow the evidence of the testimonies before us. When we seek to draw conclusions, however, the case, like many similar ones, reveals other and at first sight rather baffling aspects. If so many details were altered in the rendition of this one prototype, without any regard whatsoever to the original action, meaning, and even the sex of the model, why was a prototype employed in the first place, and what was felt to be prototypic about it? Obviously neither the subject matter, nor even the statue as a whole was considered significant in itself. What remained as a possible object of interest was a formal element of construction: a certain quality of contortion, of the kind that, one generation later, in the lingo used by the profession would have been called a *figura serpen-*

FIGURE 1. Leonardo da Vinci, *Leda and the Swan,* ca. 1504-1506, pen and ink drawing over chalk, and wash

tinata.[5] This structural principle Leonardo seems to have rediscovered in the ancient statue and used for his own purpose. A process of imitation was in fact involved, but carried out in the freest spirit. As so often in the practice of the Renaissance, it implied one artist's comment on the art of another—detached, critical if appreciative, and original.

At this point a more basic problem must be faced, namely the question of what place we are willing to concede, in the creation of a work of art, to an act of imita-

FIGURE 2. (at left) *Crouching Venus*, III cent. B.C. (?), marble
FIGURE 3. (below) Leonardo da Vinci, *St. John the Baptist*, ca. 1509-1512, panel painting

tion—any kind of imitation. The question seems to have acquired a special urgency in recent times since by modern standards, in the opinion of most people, creation and imitation are held to be mutually exclusive. The origin of this notion and the reasons for its latter-day popularity cannot be traced here, but a doubt may at least be raised whether it can stand scrutiny if confronted with the data of common experience. Our modern society has a tendency to invest the terms "creative" or "to create" with a high if somewhat mystical prestige. In the fashionable language of today the artist who "creates"—it hardly seems to matter what—is thereby assigned the role of a vicarious hero or saint who achieves what the common person cannot: he has freed himself from social indebtedness and lives by his own spiritual resources, not responsible to anyone but himself. As a creator, he is thought to be exempt from the drudgery oppressing other men who merely work. Similarly in educational theory "creative" and "creativeness" have become household words signifying the gift of free "self-expression," often with an overtone of opposition to rational thought, or to knowledge thought and learned. In passing, we may notice a rather remarkable discrepancy in these two different applications of the term. The one stresses the exceptional and charismatic character of creation while the other instead offers a universalistic interpretation, creativeness seen as a common gift of human nature in its state of intellectual innocence. Yet both schools of thought are apt to agree in postulating a state of complete freedom from outside influences, or to call it so, complete intellectual autonomy, as a necessary condition of the creative mind.

The essential loneliness of the creative act shall not be contested here. It is a fact, and one not true of the arts alone but of any other human accomplishment dependent on inspired thinking. It is also true that creativeness cannot be taught. If the academic methods have often failed in this respect, they are not alone to blame. What must be questioned is the postulate of total originality, so often joined or tacitly implied, with the current conceptions of creative work. Not only is this an abstraction which can have no place in reality as we know it; it is hardly a desirable abstraction, even, for it separates the person who for himself tries to realize the ideal, from the very materials on which the mind is obliged to operate. The point is that creativeness must in no way be restricted, and that any definition of it which tends to limit its potential range is harmful. Neither acquired knowledge, as opposed to intuition, nor awareness of the accomplishments of others, nor even imitation can be excluded beforehand from the domain of creation. The crux is not imitation itself, but its pedestrian uses; it is not incompatible with originality. Language, one of our most powerful instruments of creation, is acquired by imitation; so are the standards of excellence to which one's work aspires. In brief, imitation can be active, original, and creative, as the history of the arts has amply shown. In the face of the strictures to which modern criticism inclines, it would seem wiser to reconcile ourselves to the fact that there are instances in art where

83

imitation does freely convert itself into creation, and when it should not only be called a pardonable sin but no sin at all. The sentence in the preface to Kierkegaard's *The Sickness unto Death* may well be re-written for the arts: "From the artist's point of view everything, absolutely everything should serve for creation. The sort of thinking which is not in the last resort creative is precisely for that reason sterile."[6] This, I think, includes an artist's dealings with the art of others.

EXTRA-ACADEMIC CLASSICISM

THE opposition to academic art is about as old as the academies themselves. It was chiefly carried forward by artists, that is, professionals, both inside and outside the academic walls. There is no need here to recapitulate the controversy as it developed over the centuries, centering at first in demands for a greater choice of academically admissible subjects and eventually becoming aligned with the nineteenth-century currents, both apparently anti-classical, of romanticism and realism. This debate and most of its arguments, once so hotly contested, are now past history. In the arts the term "academic" has become rather generally discredited. It carries the connotations of art made by rules and conventions, and obedient to obsolete canons: the opposite of "creative." The contemporary position is probably still best summarized in the indictment made by Picasso in a conversation of 1935 which begins: "Academic training in beauty is a sham."[7]

Thus the existence of an art which is not academic, even actively anti-academic, has long been an accepted fact. All the art termed "modern," in contrast to mere contemporary, would be so classified. Less known is another fact, equally important here: that during the past two centuries classicism has had an extra-academic history of its own, which also led to far-reaching results. This latter revolution started in artistic criticism rather than art itself. It ended by affecting severely the meaning of "classical," as a critical term. The line dividing the old from the new runs between the early and the later writings of J. G. Winckelmann, who started out in the academic vocabulary with an essay on the imitation of the ancients, and ended with a blueprint of a history of ancient art interspersed with descriptions of individual works that exhibit a very personal, sometimes astonishing vividness. It is these descriptions, especially, which indicate the trend. They provide a foretaste of that romantic realism which subsequently became one of the cornerstones of modernism, insofar as it seeks the truth of our lives in vital experience rather than in the formalizations of reason.[8] The immediate impact of these events on art was slight, but in classical scholarship changes of outlook ensued which proved to be of more than merely specialistic interest. The paradox came about that classicism was not incapable of undergoing a romantic phase, and did so about 1800. Goethe expressed the same paradox by the oxymoron of a *Klassische Walpurgisnacht*, where the spooks of Greek fiction join their Nordic relations in a very unclassical witches' sabbath. Underlying the upheaval was a new attitude—realistic in its critical-historical method, romantic in its appreciation—toward the content of such testimonies as Greek tragedy and myth. Its most cherished discovery was the significance of that primitivism from which, as from a collective subconscious, arose the symbols and apparent monstrosities of the Greek myth.[9] The conscious and realistic insight into the human condition, as portrayed in the crimes and errors of tragic action, had as its deeper source the dark memories of ancient folk tales, on which the peculiar lucidity of the Greek thought imposed itself. At least one of the roots of modernism must be traced to this intellectual revolution in the core of the classical tradition itself, which amounted to no less than a recognition of the essentially unclassic matters to be found in so many ancient themes. From here started the modern interpretation of the Greek myths and indeed, of all myth, as a form of symbolic expression. By the end of the century the anthropological school founded by Sir J. Frazer expounded the world-wide affiliations, and inherent primitivism, of the classical myths. And another unbroken line of search and sympathetic interests leads from the philological studies of the early nineteenth century, the work of men like Welcker, Kreutzer, and Bachofen, to the philosophies of Schelling and Nietzsche, and to the psychologies of Freud and Jung.

Interestingly enough, this is also the period when the term "classical" first came into general use. The eighteenth century spoke of the ancients, or of *la belle antiquité.* From eighteen hundred on we hear more often of the "classical antiquity." Clearly the word meant first of all "Greek and Roman," but it also carried from the start the connotations of something exemplary, or worthy of imitation, and as such it was apt to develop into a true term of criticism. In the latter sense, however, it required definition. For if the term was used selectively, postulating that certain things deserved to be called classical in contrast to others which did not, then questions were bound to arise as to what were, in actuality, the manifestations of the classical, and what criteria should be used to recognize this quality wherever it might be found. Not only did the new historical studies raise a doubt of whether everything Greek and Roman must indiscriminately be called classical, if classical was at the same time a distinctive term of artistic criticism. More important still, the possibility presented itself that a classical quality might well reside in unfamiliar phenomena, and even outside the conventionally established realm of classicism. The new science of history, unlike the historical thinking of the preceding centuries, was not inclined to consider the past chiefly for its didactic value, as a moral fable illustrating human vices and virtues. Instead it set out to describe the past as a texture of events which at one time, together, had formed a living present. The analogous tendency in criticism was to regard the art of the past not merely as a demonstration of aesthetic principles but as an expression both of vital experience and a certain way of life.

One consequence of these developments is of immediate interest here. Following the changing sensibilities of the age, artists began to look for symptoms of the classical outside the contexts in which these qualities were habitually thought to occur and, on occasion, even among cultures beyond the frontiers of the Western, Christian civilization. Thus Delacroix delighted in the native life of northern Africa as a living antiquity. Later Gauguin incorporated academic-classical, as well as Egyptian, reminiscences with his representations of Tahitian women, thereby professing that he had found the quality of the classical in its natural state.[10] The discovery for modern art of primitive aesthetics and exotic themes was, of course, an intellectual event of many facets, but it certainly did not exclude the academic habit of imitation, however unacademically applied. Yet as the objects of imitation changed, so did the demonstrations of that certain quality or attitude of art, which experience and judgment compel us to call classical. Thus it is useful to remember that the modern drive toward the primitive and exotic, which so often turned its opposition to academic traditions, had at the same time, as one constituent element, a desire to infuse with a new vitality the notion of the classical. In the wake of these developments "classical," as a term of criticism, reached its modern stage of significance. We now treat it as an open proposition, the conditions of which may be fulfilled by an unspecified number of actual instances. It is still apt to suggest references to past art, but not necessarily to Greek and Roman only. The line of continuity, of a classical style, leads well beyond the Italian Renaissance into more recent periods and even the present. Thus the term has lost something of the categorical precision which it had once possessed in academic classicism. Yet in other respects its selective function has been strengthened, imparting to it the qualitative precision of a critical concept which is well known by experience, if not by theory. Classical, in this sense, is a certain way of doing things or of presenting them. It can be actualized in unfamiliar forms and recognized in unexpected circumstances, by the analogy of other phenomena previously found "classical."

Independence goes hand in hand with isolation. The growing independence and critical isolation of the concept of classical in modern art can be seen in the two standing women in the center of Picasso's *Demoiselles d'Avignon* of 1907 (fig. 4), especially the figure second from the left in the foreground. Certainly a classical reminiscence has here been willfully transferred to alien and uncongenial surroundings. The pose is conventionally academic: any studio model could be so posed. Its line of ancestry goes back to Ingres' *La Source* and Goujon (fig. 5), if not to the Greeks. Immediate precedents occur in the works of Cézanne (e.g., fig. 6); there, already, we find the same motive unclassically distorted.[11] In such isolation the memory of the classical like any other fact of life may well evoke very different reactions—admiration, hatred, or ridicule. There is something frightening and savage about Picasso's figures with their stupid seriousness and hysterically opened eyes. But regardless of our passing moods, veering between acceptance and rebellion, the existence and power of a classical configuration has once more become acknowledged and confirmed as a matter of experience. A persiflage perhaps, twisted and fragmented but of unquestionable reality, it has nevertheless been turned into a demonstration of classicism on the existential level.

THE NEOCLASSICISM OF PICASSO

To BRING this discussion into focus, some observations on the neoclassic art of Picasso are in order. The matter is of symtomatic importance. Art of a neoclassic character can be found in the work of Picasso at various times. It was especially frequent in the twenty-year span from 1917 to 1937. Perhaps the contacts with Diaghilev and the Russian Ballet set off the trend: after all, the ballet was then itself a very neoclassic form of art. But one must also remember that the interest in a classical style, on a modern level, was at that time not limited to any single artist. The 1920's saw a veritable revival of classicism in all its arts, mostly centered in the Paris School.[12] About the same time Stravinsky composed his classical music, and a deliberately cultivated, rather neoclassic style prevailed with writers such as Paul Valéry. and André Gide, to name only two of its exponents. The neoclassic art of Picasso follows the same general trend. One symptom is common to this entire category, which comprises a sizable portion of his total production. Its classicism is

overt, not latent or transmuted as so often in other periods of Picasso's works. The compositions in the neoclassic style, of which there are many, were first of all
intended to look classical. We may say that their classicism is their principal theme; it is also the ostensible
reason for their existence. Again they assert the phenomenon of the classical, isolating it from other modes of
art as a verifiable fact of experience. Thus by demon-
strating the practicability of a classical style they also
define it. Implicitly they answer a question: what is
classical about the classical?

The question of course was not new. It is on the contrary inherent in the classical tradition on every level,
especially in the academic program of the arts. Ultimately the source of doubt lay with those portions of
Greek art itself, which in retrospect were labeled classical. For Greek art was apt to fuse abstract principles of
structure with an appearance of naturalness which later
has often seemed enigmatic and, in effect, has often
proved misleading. The tendency to apply a naturalistic
interpretation to classical art is already noticeable in
Renaissance thinking;[13] it has increased since. Yet it is
obviously difficult to assess fairly the share of naturalistic
intentions in the formation of the Greek, classical style.
Therefore the Renaissance and post-Renaissance insistence on a naturalistic interpretation of that art, as if an
accurate rendition of nature were its chief asset, created
a critical dilemma which permeates all reflections on art
from the seventeenth century on. The formal independence and formative power of classical art were strongly

Photographie Giraudon

FIGURE 4. (upper right) Picasso, *Les Demoiselles d'Avignon*, 1907, oil on canvas
FIGURE 5. (left) Goujon, nymph from *The Fountain of the Innocents*, 1547-9
FIGURE 6. (lower right) Cézanne, *The Judgment of Paris*, 1883-5, oil on canvas

appreciated; at the same time, rather paradoxically, these very qualities were held to be derived from a close attention to nature. The wish to harmonize art and nature, in theory and if possible in practice, was ever-present in the aesthetics of classicism.[14] In practice, the academic tradition for the most part took it for granted that both were in full accord; there could be no possible contrast between perfect art and perfect nature. Accordingly in the art schools, casts of the famed models of art mingled with those from nature: human hands, feet, or arms. In the academic tradition the two categories were not generally considered as rivals, not even when in the course of the nineteenth century doubts began to be raised regarding the alleged naturalism of classical art, and in another camp the term "naturalism" came to signify a program of art in outright opposition to academic classicism.

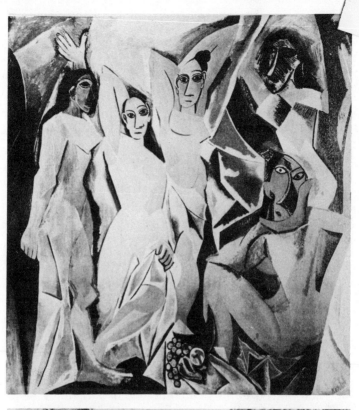

Plaster casts, those adjuncts of academic training, are not absent from the work of Pablo Picasso. We find drawings after the reclining *Theseus* from the east pediment of the Parthenon, or from Michelangelo's *Dawn*, as well as from casts of human limbs.[15] The majority of them represent very early studies, to be sure, the precocious work of a boy eleven and twelve years old. This fact does not impair their testimonial value, as illustrations of an academic training which this artist, for one, does not seem to have easily forgotten. Clearly the neoclassical compositions after 1917 raise the academic question again. But they argue their case on a different level of comprehension and with a new answer in the making. In these compositions the quality of the classical becomes defined as pure form, quite divorced from any naturalistic intent, in the sense of a direct pictorial record of natural accidentals. It is shown to be a result of styling, and indeed to be a certain mode of art, an autonomous world of form. The demonstration amounts to a discovery. By dint of this discovery classicism is recognized to be an ally rather than an opponent of that trend in modern art which restores to the artist his power over the natural data, and his unimpaired responsibility for the work of his creation. The essence of the classical is form, runs the argument here.[16]

As I perceive it the demonstration of this tenet occurs in three distinct ways in the neoclassic art of Picasso. In a number of instances, especially in the years 1920 to 1923, the human figures, mostly women, assume an air of simple massiveness and a quiet, at times somewhat

FIGURE 7. Picasso, *Women at the Fountain*, 1921, oil on canvas

stolid monumentality reminiscent of the material density of sculpture. The details of their heads are broadly spaced, with eyes, eyebrows and lips sharply drawn as if they were carved in stone. Indeed they often look like portrayals of statuary rather than live flesh. In cases such as these, the interpretation of form is clearly sculptural

95

(e.g., fig 7). By contrast, in another class of works, examples of which are frequent among Picasso's drawings and graphics from the twenties, and still persist during the early thirties, the classicality of style rests in the purity of outlines without shading (e.g., fig 8). In these compositions the classical quality is expressed by the calligraphic rhythms and by the deftness and visual persuasiveness of mere design. One receives the impression that the infinitely flexible contours dematerialize the solid bodies, dissolve the density of flesh, and thus set free an immaterial quality of spirit, mood, or sheer movement. In either way, in the maternal gravity of the almost sculpted women or the virginal suppleness of the drawn dancers and bathers, the work of art asserts the primacy of form over content. Both modes argue the subordination of nature to a rule of art, superbly managed.

The third and perhaps most interesting aspect of this revived classicism is the concept of image which it also incorporates. For in the neoclassic compositions by Picasso the criteria of the classical have not been restricted to the descriptive qualities of mass and line. The same formal, a-naturalistic interpretation pertains to the design of figures in their entirety, as patterned representations of a certain stance or motion. The formalization of expressive human postures of course was very much a concern of classical and later, of Renaissance art. It was the ultimate answer to the principal problem of all ancient arts, namely, the creation of images. An image so understood constitutes by definition a created, that is, an artificial thing. It is also a wholeness, a configuration of parts or to use another technical term, a *Gestalt*. Therefore it cannot be derived from natural data by direct observation only. It represents rather a condensation of experience, cast into a memorable form. In terms of art, it constitutes a definitive formal statement on something in reality. As such, any image tends to isolate its object.

The neoclassic art of Picasso entirely turns on a concept of image of this kind. It represents a world of fancy, of created images. In these freely invented compositions chance has no place. References to earlier art are frequent, if more or less veiled. As in the Renaissance, images are treated as visual formulae capable of multiple variations. In fact it is a characteristic trait of the classicism of Picasso that Renaissance reminiscences occur hardly less often than references to ancient art. In either case the interest centers in the rendition of individual figures and their groupings. The spaciousness and freedom given to these figures and their actions mark them as classical; this would also be true of those related images and groups whose nimble postures recall the classical ballet. The ballet, likewise, aims at transforming the motions of live bodies into artifices. From this classicism which so deliberately fosters the formal independence of the image an air of naturalness is not excluded. But it is recognized as a concept of the mind which art must define, not illustrate. Even when these images deal with facts of natural experience, it remains clear that their native habitat is in art, not nature.

The repertory of ancient art underlying this modern

FIGURE 9. Picasso, *Head of Woman in Profile*, 1921, pastel

exploration of classicism is neither large nor conspicuous. After all, the issue at hand was a very general one. Almost anything classical could serve for demonstration. Heads of women often recall the Venus of Milo, especially in profile (figs. 7, 9, 10). Another head representing a young boy (fig. 11), reminiscences of which recur several times in varying contexts, may likewise hark back

FIGURE 10. (above) *Venus of Milo* (detail of head), latter part of IV cent. B.C. (?), marble

FIGURE 11. (upper right) Picasso, *Head of a Young Man*, 1923, conté crayon

FIGURE 12. (lower right) Picasso, *Olga Picasso*, 1923, Chinese ink

to a classical model, probably a Roman portrait. Both types were also transferred to portraits of living persons where the resemblance may be acknowledged as an intended comparison (fig. 12). Among these women bathers a standing figure seen from the back, repeated in a number of instances, resembles an ancient Venus of the Medici type (fig. 13, left). A cast or photograph may have been the remembered model. All these antiquities, of course, were standbys of the academic tradition. In addition, the manner of drawing details as well as entire figures at times shows the artist's interest in other products of classical art which were not so commonly utilized in academic practice: objects such as Greek white *lekythoi,* or Etruscan mirrors with their engraved outlines.

More unusual, as a case of classical survival, is the history of a type of running—sometimes dancing—woman with head thrown back in wild abandon, which made its first appearance in the work of Picasso about 1920. Its classical antecedents are the figures of Creusa in Roman sarcophagi representing the story of Medea (fig. 14). The type, a highly patterned and expressive formula, had already attracted the attention of Renaissance artists. In what way it entered the work of Picasso I cannot say. Even if the similarity were entirely accidental it would still indicate a genuine kinship between his grasp of a classical form and the free adoption of classical inventions practiced in the Renaissance. In Picasso's art the best known example is probably the woman nearer the observer, on the drop curtain for *The Blue Train* of 1924 (*Two Women Running on a Beach,*

FIGURE 8. (above) Picasso, *Bathers*, 1921, pencil

FIGURE 13. (below) Picasso, *Group of Female Nudes*, 1921, pastel

figs. 8, 15). But other instances can be found as well. An earlier variant of considerable interest occupies the background of the *Three Women Bathers* of 1920 (fig. 16). There the figure appears distorted, if in a rather meaningful way. While she moves swiftly into the open spaces of sky and sea, her head, arm, and shoulders, which are thrust forward, grow rapidly smaller as an airplane in flight seems to grow smaller while it moves away from us. The patterned image, "woman in rapid motion," thus acquires new connotations of time and space, or of motion into space. In fact it is the image-formula itself which here gives rise to the creation of such variants; also, being committed to its stable form, it is apt to point up the dilemma inherent in any restive formalization of transient movements. The assumed, formal identity of the image with its object is properly incompatible with the temporal succession of changes which the object undergoes in motion. Thus the running figure in the *Three Women Bathers* may well be described as a study of identity in motion. It is important, nevertheless, to realize that this rather ingenious demonstration was based on a pre-existing type of image of which the example at hand is only a special variant. In this one instance, one must call the motivation and execution of the variant specifically modern. But comparable formal variations of pre-established figural inventions, though created for different reasons, were no rarity in other, earlier kinds of western art. Usually they appear in the wake of a prevailingly classical style. At all events, whenever they occur, they give notice of a formal rather than naturalistic interpretation of the classical phenomenon. The first symptoms of such a state of affairs can already be recognized in Greek art after the period of the Parthenon. And formal variation is only one step from formal distortion. The latter fact becomes clear in provincial Roman (fig. 17) and late classical art and again at the close of the Renaissance in the art now often called "mannerism." With Picasso this matter is of crucial importance. The logical sequence from image to formal variation and then to distortion became a proper characteristic of his art quite early in his career. The story of the wild dancer, likewise, has not yet ended. We find her again in the large canvas of 1925, *The Three Dancers* (fig. 18), where she occupies the space left of the center. More frantic than ever, wildly distorted and insanely grinning, she establishes a strange contrast to the solemn Egyptian on the opposite side of the painting.

THE IMPORTANCE OF MEANING

THE *Three Dancers* cannot of course be described as a neoclassic work in any regular sense of the word. Not only are their distortions too violent for that; another and probably more decisive reason is the different relation, in this painting, between the work of art and its subject matter. As a rule a high degree of objectivity, that is, detachment from subjects represented, characterizes the modern concept of classicism. Thus in Picasso's neoclassic art conventional themes are frequent which, like

FIGURE 14. *Medea Sarcophagus*, Antonine period, Roman Empire

Women Bathers, require a minimum of specific or personal interpretation. In these presentations art constitutes a world of objective form and objective phenomena. By contrast the *Three Dancers* must be called a rather subjective work, charged with connotations of personal meaning. In the art of Picasso after 1925, the latter was the rising trend. In its wake the thematic importance of the work of art became vastly increased, even when generic titles such as *Still Life* or *Seated Woman* were retained. Up to this point the neoclassic compositions tended to minimize content or at least to reduce it, in each instance, to a 'state of monumental singleness in

FIGURE 15. Picasso, *Two Women Running on a Beach,* 1922, gouache on board

keeping with the isolating force of each image. In the new style, on the contrary, contents mattered a great deal, and each subsequent work became a fresh demonstration of the symbolical powers of art. As these discoveries rapidly progressed, and forms became ever more freely exploited to create contents of countless surprises, even the classical reminiscences turned into personal symbols of a haunting if uncertain meaning.

In the years following 1925 Picasso painted a series of still-lifes, many of which include academic equipment. Sculptured heads of more or less classical appearance stand on tables amongst sundry objects, all allusions to

105

FIGURE 16. Picasso, *Three Bathers*, 1920, oil on board

the artist's studio. For the first time, plaster casts of human arms and hands join the sculptured heads. Also the torso of the standing Venus returns, if only in rather surrealistic compositions restricted to the media of drawing and graphic art. At times it is confronted with a new character, the warrior: a helmeted head, perhaps derived from Etruscan bronzes (fig. 19). To relate the story of this imagery would be a very entertaining task, but this lies beyond the scope of the present essay.[17] In the rather unclassical style of these compositions the academic remnants stand curiously alone, as if their strangeness were deliberately emphasized. No longer do they serve as a demonstration of form. Instead they are treated as semi-animated objects; they represent the memories of a past not wholly dead, yet remembered more often than not with uneasy feelings of mockery and anger. About the same time the ancient myth of the bull-man began to interest Picasso, and this interest led him after 1932 to the beautiful series of the Minotaur-compositions.[18] But here, again, the emphasis is on content, and on the uncanny persuasiveness of the mythical symbols. The casts and statuary, the formal monitors of academic memory, hardly entered into these mythical fantasies. Only in *Guernica*, painted 1937, were some of the familiar academic paraphernalia of Picasso's art assembled once more, not to be shown again thereafter; it is as if they had perished in the holocaust. The head, the plaster arm lie shattered on the ground. Above, almost in contrast to them, appears the only truly classical detail of this large painting, terrible in its bleak grandeur: the face of the woman with the lamp.

The iconography of the painting now known as *Guernica* obviously represents a special problem, beyond our boundaries here.[19] We shall emphasize, however, that by the time this work came into being the existence of a modern style of classicism was already an accomplished fact. We can rest the case right there. Only, to sum up our findings, it may be useful to add a brief appraisal of the conditions in which a style of classicism, of any kind, must be expected to operate if it appears at all in contemporary art. In the first place it can only be one of several, possible choices. Secondly, the definition

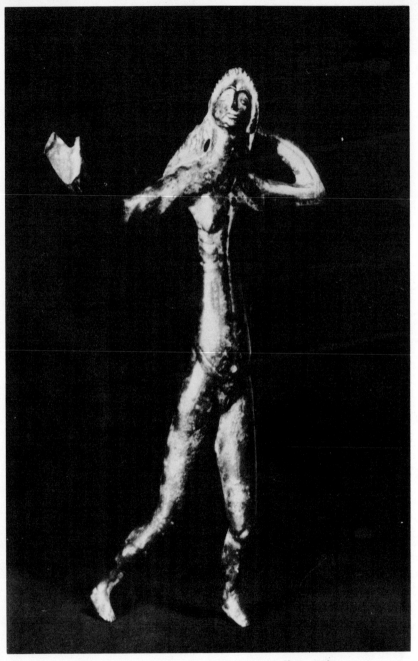

FIGURE 17. *Dancer* from Neury-en-Sullias, Celtic

FIGURE 18. Picasso, *Three Dancers*, 1925, oil on canvas

of the classical quality remains wide open. Even though we are confident that the quality exists we are at a loss to describe its symptoms definitely. The tendency has long been to apply the term ever more broadly: we now hear about "classical jazz" or "classical abstractionism." This condition reflects the fact that the term has lost its moorings in the academic tradition. It also implies that the quality of the classical can be recognized in unfamiliar manifestations, both of form and content, and that it is not incompatible with newness. More than ever, "classical" is now an autonomous term of artistic criticism. As such it is not defined by rules, though it can be demonstrated by examples.

To the neoclassic art of Picasso which offers the most consistent modern contribution to the problem, the formal, not naturalistic, interpretation must be considered basic. This re-evaluation of classicism had far-reaching effects on his art, not merely confined to those compositions in which a classical style openly prevails. First of all it greatly strengthened the concept of image which had been Picasso's concern all along, and must indeed be considered a constituent of his art. It also imparted to his images that isolating force which identifies and singles out its objects (as in the formula by Gertrude Stein: a rose is a rose etc.). Thirdly, and this perhaps constitutes the most important result of his classicism, it established the independence of the image as a formal configuration which is capable of infinite variations and thereby, with each new pattern, may create new connotations of meaning. Picasso is a master of formal order, yet the terms we use to describe formal context in a painting such as space, or composition, are rarely applicable in their conventional sense to his work after 1920. This is so, because he habitually works from the formal configurations, or images, toward context; he does not subordinate images to their settings. Though the images may enter into formal connections with one another, it is they which create the surface pattern of the painting. Interest focuses on the images as essentially disconnected, self-contained formal inventions. Thus the formal context follows from the images; it does not precede or dominate them. In the same manner, in these same compositions, meaning follows form instead of preceding it. Yet an artist who so expressly founds his art on the incorruptible force of images, and so clearly creates his images from isolating and defining forms, must be said to practice a classical principle however unclassical the uses may be to which the precept is often put. In the light of these considerations the neoclassic art of Picasso assumes an aspect of lasting importance for all of his work. It stands for much more than merely a passing episode.

One final remark about the coherence, over the centuries, of the concept of art which we now call the classical. There can be little doubt that in the wake of the Renaissance, and especially in the subsequent academic tradition, this coherence was brought about mostly by the direct study of definite ancient models. Thus in the case of Leonardo it is a safe assumption that the artist actually knew one of the surviving copies, whether statue or statuette, of the Hellenistic *Crouching Venus*, and applied this knowledge to his own work. Modern conditions, on the contrary, are likely to make the relation between a classical reminiscence and its possible source much more problematic. This must be so partly because contemporary classicism can operate on so many different levels of meaning, either purely thematic or purely formal; in each case the outcome may be far remote from any actual classical prototype. Moreover in our society there exists another rather perplexing circumstance which is quite peculiarly modern: it is the enormously broadened distribution of knowledge owing to the contemporary mass media of print and photography. One example will be sufficient to make the importance of this matter clear at once. The same crouching figure which apparently pleased Leonardo also pleased Picasso. We find a nude figure of similar cast, varied several times, in *La comédie humaine*, the book of drawings Picasso published in 1954 (fig. 20). A Cupid who cavorts in the air above the crouching girl, hiding his face behind a masque, adds a touch of mockery and allegory to this little fantasy which among its companion drawings seems a rather lighthearted intermezzo, but also quite a classical one. To ask here for a definite source or prototype would clearly be meaningless. The possible sources are too many. Any photograph in a book or magazine could have served as a reminder. Moreover, this little composition, which has every appearance of a happy improvisation, can only be called classical in a very broad sense. Classical indeed was the starting point

FIGURE 20. Picasso, *Nymph and Masked Cupid* from *The Human Comedy*, 1954, ink drawing

of its imagery: the idea of the Cupid with the unbecoming masque, and the formal pattern of the crouching figure. Either can be traced to ancient art; either was known to the Renaissance. Their iconographic history after the sixteenth century has not yet been assembled.

If it were attempted, examples would come from every level of taste, the more ambitious as well as the popular and decorative, including engraved illustrations in books. The drawing by Picasso, coming after a long series of imitations, adaptations, and variations, occupies a place where the question of how many examples of a type, and which ones, had by chance attracted the attention of an artist, must seem rather irrelevant. Clearly no single statue or ready composition was here imitated, though a classical image was evoked, however freely.

Since their classical origin, many different associations have accrued to the images which once formed the core of the academic tradition. The turn toward modernism occurred when Cézanne applied to them his own new interpretations, often surprising and cryptically personal. For the young artists around 1906, in many instances, his figural compositions with classical overtones such as the numerous *Bathers* came to form the most immediate link with the past.[20] Progressively, in modern conditions, the notion of the classical thus became detached from its original exemplars, growing diffuse and anonymous rather than specific. It also became highly variable. The drawings by Picasso referred to above, together with their classical forms introduce clearly non-classical features, such as the rendition of the pubic hair which resembles the manner used in Japanese wood cuts. In Picasso's art such a fusion of foreign reminiscences is not unusual. It does, however, throw a light on the status of the classical image formulae in modern surroundings. It underlines their foreignness. After all, in a time so dominated by naturalistic thought as ours, a classical form is also apt to look alien. In this respect, at least, it is on a level with the exotic. For all that the term "classical" is still applicable, nor would any other description fit these drawings by Picasso. What emerges from all our considerations is the circumstance that, while the idea of a classical style can hardly claim ultimate validity with us, it still signifies one of the irreducible elements of art. As such it can be, and is, reactivated freely, with a negative or positive prefix as the case may be. But wherever in modern art we find a statement in a classical vein, we know that it can no longer be regarded as the natural result of a unified tradition. It always represents a judicious choice.

NOTES

1 W. Barrett, *Irrational Man* (New York, 1958), p. 41.

2 Academies: N. Pevsner, *Academies of Art Past and Present* (Cambridge, Eng., 1940); Sir Joshua Reynolds, *Discourses on Art*, ed. R. R. Wark (San Marino, Calif., 1959), introduction, pp. xv ff. Cf. also M. C. Bradley, Jr., "The Academic Point of View," *Technical Studies in the Fine Arts*, VII (1938-39), pp. 139 ff. Post-Renaissance Classicism: J. Seznec, *Essais sur Diderot* (Paris, 1957); W. Pach, *The Classical Tradition in Modern Art* (London, 1959); M. Praz, *Gusto neoclassico* (Naples, 1959).

3 For a characteristic instance see Reynolds, *Discourses on Art*, "Discourse III," pp. 46 ff. To refer to famous ancient statuary by short names such as "the torso," "the Apollo," was common academic usage ultimately derived from Vasari. The reader or hearer was expected to know that "the torso" meant

the Belvedere torso, "the Apollo" the Belvedere Apollo, etc.

4 O. J. Brendel, "Borrowings of Ancient Art in Titian," *Art Bulletin*, XXXVII (1955), pp. 113 ff.; bibliography, p. 114, note 2. Add R. Krautheimer, *Lorenzo Ghiberti* (Princeton, 1956), pp. 277 ff.; Phyllis Pray Bober, *Drawings after the Antique by Amico Aspertini: Sketchbooks in the British Museum* (London, 1957), pp. 96 ff., 104 ff.; C. C. Vermeule, III, "The dal Pozzo-Albani Drawings of Classical Antiquities in the British Museum," *Transactions of the American Philosophical Society*, L, part 5 (Philadelphia, 1960).

5 Giovanni da Bologna later showed a marked preference for the same figure, obviously for the identical reason. Since then the *Crouching Venus* has occupied a stable place in the academic tradition; R. Lullies, *Die kauernde Aphrodite* (Munich, 1954), pp. 7 ff.

6 For the original wording of this passage see S. Kierkegaard, *Fear and Trembling; The Sickness unto Death*, tr. by W. Lowrie (Garden City, N. Y., 1954), p. 142.

7 Quoted fully in the following essay, p. 138.

8 J. J. Winckelmann, *Gedanken über die Nachahmung der griechischen Werke in der Malerey und Bildhauerkunst* (Dresden, 1755). Winckelmann, *Geschichte der Kunst des Alterthums* (Dresden, 1764). Cf. O. J. Brendel, "Prolegomena to a Book on Roman Art," *Memoirs of the American Academy in Rome*, XXI (1953), pp. 17 ff.

9 See the following essay, pp. 140 ff. and note 15; especially the studies cited in note 15, by G. Highet and W. Müri. Also the article by Fiske Kimball, "Romantic Classicism in Architecture," *Gazette des Beaux Arts*, XXV, 1944, pp. 95 ff., is relevant here; and readers of A. Gide will remember his brilliant if unfinished essay, "Considérations sur la mythologie grecque," first published in 1919, reprinted in his *Oeuvre complète*, IX (Bruges, 1935), pp. 147 ff.

10 Delacroix: W. Pach, "Introduction," *The Journal of Eugene Delacroix* (New York, 1948), pp. 20 ff. Pach, "Le Classicisme de Delacroix," *La Revue des Arts*, II (1952), pp. 109 ff. H. Fegers, "Delacroix und die Antike," *Form und Inhalt: Kunstgeschichtliche Studien* [Festschrift für Otto Schmitt], (Stuttgart, 1950), pp. 297 ff.

Gauguin: R. Rey, *La renaissance du sentiment classique* (Paris, 1931), pp. 60 ff. Fusions of classical with exotic elements occur especially in the latest works of Gauguin, from 1899 till 1902. See Th. Rousseau, Jr., "Gauguin," *Catalog*, exhibitions at Art Institute of Chicago and Metropolitan Museum of Art, New York, (Chicago, 1959), no. 64, *Two Tahitian Women;* no. 68, *The Call;* no. 69, *Horsemen on the Beach.*

11 J. Golding, "The 'Demoiselles d'Avignon'," *The Burlington Magazine*, C (1958), pp. 155 ff. With regard to Cézanne, see G. Berthold, *Cézanne und die alten Meister* (Stuttgart, 1958), pp. 38 ff. and figs. 35-55. See also the supplement and review of Berthold: Th. Reff, *Art Bulletin*, XLII (1960), pp. 145 ff. Cf. Th. Reff, "Cézanne: The Enigma of the Nude," *Art News*, LVIII (Nov. 1959), pp. 26 ff. A similar figure occurs also in Matisse's famous painting of 1906, *Le bonheur de vivre.*

12 Also in Paris, in 1921, the painter Gino Severini published his programmatic book, *Du Cubisme au Classicisme (Esthétique du compas et du nombre);* for this reminder, as well as much valuable help in compiling this bibliography, I thank my assistant, Stanford Anderson. For further details cf. O. Schürer, "Der Neoklassizismus in der jüngsten französischen Malerei," *Jahrbuch für Philologie*, I (1925), pp. 427 ff.

13 E. Panofsky, *Renaissance and Renascences in Western Art* (Stockholm, 1960), pp. 19 ff.

14 The contrast between the conflicting ideals of "natural" and "classical," and a desire to reconcile the two, already appears in Vasari; Panofsky, *Renaissance and Renascences in Western Art*, especially pp. 31 ff. In order to trace this situation in later classicism where the testimonies abound, it will be advisable to distinguish between the practical level of the art academies on the one side and theoretical criticism on the other. The already cited discourses by Reynolds may be regarded as representative of the former; the unresolved contradictions in Winckelmann's esthetics typify the critical dilemma. Cf. my "Prolegomena" cited above, note 8, pp. 17 ff. and 43 ff. Further bibliography in the studies by Bagnani and Müri cited in the following essay, note 15. I should add that,

while the dichotomy continues virtually unchanged throughout the eighteenth and nineteenth centuries, its harmonization in actual works of art vary considerably. The probable explanation lies in the increasingly scientific interpretation of the first element of the dichotomy, the term "natural." The second element, the concept of "classical," remained comparatively constant until ca. 1800. Yet it had to be combined with a progressively stricter, scientifically oriented demand of natural verisimilitude. In this sense the classicism of David, for example, was more modern than that of Poussin; indeed, I should call it a scientific classicism. For all that it must still be considered an outcome of the academic tradition; cf. F. Antal, "Reflections on Classicism and Romanticism," *The Burlington Magazine*, LXVI (1935), pp. 159 ff. The spurious remark often ascribed to Cézanne that Poussin must be remade from nature merely constitutes a more recent restatement of the same dilemma: the dilemma itself is congenital with the modern tradition of criticism. See Th. Reff, "Cézanne and Poussin," *Journal of the Warburg and Courtauld Institutes*, XXIII (1960), pp. 150 ff., for a historical critique of the above remark, alleged to Cézanne.

15 Following essay, notes 1 and 2.

16 Earlier, formal interpretations of classicism: A. E. Brinckmann, "The Classical Temper of French Art," *Formes*, No. 20 (1931), pp. 173 ff.

17 Following essay, p. 138 ff. and illustrations.

18 Following essay, pp. 133 ff. and illustrations.
   Picasso's use of mythical symbols: H. Bolliger, *Picasso for Vollard* (New York, 1956), p. xii; M. Jardot, *Pablo Picasso: Drawings* (New York, 1959), pp. viii ff.

19 See following essay, especially pp. 125 ff.

20 P. Pool, "Sources and Backgrounds of Picasso's Art 1900-6," *The Burlington Magazine*, CI (1959), pp. 176 ff. Cézanne's *Bathers:* see bibliographical note 11, above.

FIGURE 1. Picasso, *Guernica*, May-early June, 1937, oil on canvas (11'5½" x 25'¾")

Otto J. Brendel

M Y CONTENTION here is not only that classic elements
are included in the painting, now so famous,
which Picasso first showed in the Spanish Government
Pavilion at the Paris World's Fair of 1937, and named
Guernica; but that this painting more than any other
elucidates what "classic" means, and indeed what this
term can possibly mean, in a modern work of art. For
whatever we call "classic" of course has its ultimate roots
in some ancient thought, either Greek or Latin, or in
some ancient artistic monument. But the "classic" is
also a living tradition and, as such, a part of the contemporary scene. In its modern phase tradition is no

longer concerned solely with the ancient exemplars, as was the classicism of the Renaissance. It has since acquired many new saints to worship and new models to contend with. For one thing, the Renaissance has meanwhile made its own contribution and left an unforgettable impress on the Western mind. Raphael is now a part of the classical tradition; so is the art of Poussin, of Ingres, though obviously the latter two are "classical" in a somewhat different sense. "Classical" is today confronted with, and distinct from, "neoclassic." Another complicating factor has appeared in our evaluation of the ancient materials themselves, since we have become acquainted with many facets of ancient art to which the attribute "classical" is commonly denied. Greek archaic, much Etruscan, much Roman art are "ancient" but not "classic." It is no longer possible to expound in a simple statement the role of classicism in modern thought, nor the range of its contents. One cannot even assert that the contemporary forms of classicism are always readily recognized.

Accordingly, the term "classical" has during the last century and a half tended to develop three dimensions of meaning, of rising complexity. All are aspects of the same intellectual problem. The primary function of the term was, and still is, as a synonym of "Greek and Roman," generally speaking. At the same time, "classical" retains something of a selective connotation, in the sense of "exemplary." This meaning for the most part underlies that current of contemporary thought which for the sake of brevity I have earlier called "academic." In this selective sense certain models and manners of art are "classical." The term thus acquires a rather definite if restricted content, traditionally established . Thirdly, beyond the confines of such traditionalism, the same word can also be used in a much broader sense. It then is likely to express a special quality of art and thought, a specific attitude, not easily describable by any other term, toward the forms into which we cast the human experience and toward the definition of form itself. Only in the latter sense is "classical" truly a critical term, with a postulated meaning to be actualized in many different ways. By necessity, in this sense it must also become a controversial term, dealing not with a set evaluation of ancient or of any other art but with an essential aspect of all art; exemplified chiefly but not exclusively by the arts of ancient Greece and Rome, and known by experience if not by definition. Indeed the term so understood invites constant revision and redefinition: We do not know what the "classicality of classical art" (to call it so) really is, with what nameable qualities it can be identified, nor even if it exists unless in comparison with other art, notably our own. We also leave the question open as to whether it is a desirable, let alone the supremely desirable, quality in any work of art. But we have acknowledged the fact, sustained by experience, that a work of art may incorporate the character of the classical, in its form or its spirit (see preceding article).

In the early 1890's, when Picasso's career as an artist began, the problem of the classical had already entered its triple-faced stage. As in the Renaissance the whole of ancient culture was felt to be classical, an indivisible unity, in solid contrast to the modern. On the other hand the classical trend in the contemporary arts on the whole continued the more selective academic tradition of the seventeenth century; at the same time it found itself in opposition to other currents which with more or less radicalism questioned the supremacy of the academic models, together with the aesthetic tenets underlying their selection. For a young artist in training this situation was likely to assume the concrete form of the plaster casts which were the inevitable equipment of all art schools the world over, as a trademark of the profession as well as a protestation of academic righteousness. In the practice of the schools the meaning of the term, clasical, thereby tended to become rather narrowly defined: it came to mean little more than a faithful adherence to this handful of generally recommended models and the principles thought to be incorporated in them.[1] Finally, outside the schools, the growing pace of discoveries during the nineteenth century had a decidedly anti-academic effect. This development could not fail to affect the discussions about art, even as regarded the principles of art. It was likely to shake the confidence in any facile definition of the nature of the classical; and it provided a vast body of material hitherto unknown or unnoticed, pre-Greek, primitive, and post-classical, in which—as during the early Renaissance, before the rise of the academic tradition—personal choice was again possible and rewarded by new insights. The ultimate authority of judgment and the power of aesthetic adventure was thus restored to the sensitive eye, and the case of the "classical" reopened. In this process the classical tradition came to compete with many other manifestations of art. Also, as it had for a long time, its selective formalism continued to compete with the more immediate approaches toward the description of natural experience. But, while its proclaimed models thus lost their status of supremacy as the sole guides of taste and conduct, the entire complex of classical art and thought regained the chance of being viewed afresh by curious minds, untainted with prejudice.

The work of Picasso, which is so exceptionally rich in themes and subject-matters, reflects this controversial situation rather clearly, at its various levels. Like so many other artists of his generation he, too, began by drawing from casts, as a young boy when he was still working under the guidance of his father at the Academy of La Coruña. Several of these drawings have been published, including some studies after the antique.[2] The memory of these early academic exercises returns upon occasion in much later pictures, sometimes with apparent overtones of dismay. We shall in time come back to this matter. Classical reminiscences of another type, not necessarily derived from definite'objects, have also left abundant traces in his œuvre. It is obvious that at certain times the occupation with the classic as a phenomenon of style and a special mood meant a great deal to the artist, witness the many compositions in a classical vein created during the 1920's. Frequently they are works of rather private and intimate character, including many drawings and a good deal of graphic art. Greek white *lekythoi,* engraved Etruscan mirrors, and also sculpture seem to have served as a starting point.[3] One finds in these works an expressiveness of line, rivaling the calligraphy of outline which Ingres mastered, but also new and earthier notes like the demonstration of massiveness, of healthy solidity in forms sculptured *à la grècque.* At any rate, the nature of the classical appears as the comprehensive theme of all these compositions. It becomes defined in its visual aspects, as form, not exclusively in terms of Greek or even ancient art, but always so as to make the onlooker feel that something special is at stake. Yet by 1937, the year of *Guernica,* all this was a matter of the past; and it is a strange fact in itself that so much past memory should once more be conjured up and incorporated in this large and extraordinary painting, which thus seemed from the outset destined to epitomize the end of an era, while at the same time signalizing the beginning of a new one. With these reminiscences, the images in which Picasso expressed himself at this crucial turn, we must now occupy ourselves.

Picasso's *Guernica* painting forms an intricate skein of meanings, not all equally clear but all interlocking. Before further discussion it might therefore be helpful briefly to recapitulate the preliminary facts. The Spanish Civil War was in its last, bitter stage. On the afternoon of April 28, 1937, the little Basque town of Guernica in the province of Bilbao was destroyed by an air raid, the first of its kind in our contemporary history, as events have since shown. Two days later Picasso started working. By the middle of May numerous sketches had been created, and the principal parts of the composition established. One month later, by June 15, the painting as we now know it was completed.[4]

Although painted on canvas entirely in black, white, and grey this monumental work may well be called a wall painting. It has in every respect the character of a public proclamation, in scale as well as style. Yet its terrifying imagery remains startling and inexplicable like a dream. That is to say, the signs and images are not too difficult to name, each for itself. Only their context, the way in which they relate to one another if at all, is difficult to determine. In any event, a closer acquaintance with this composition can be established only through a description of its apparent contents, and for this purpose the one given a few years ago by Alfred Barr can hardly be surpassed in its detached brevity:

One sees: at the right two women, one with arms raised before a burning house, the other rushing in toward the center of the picture; at the left a mother with a dead child, and on the ground the fragments of a warrior, one hand clutching a broken sword. At the center of the canvas is a dying horse pierced by a spear hurled from above; at the left a bull stands triumphantly surveying the scene. Above, to the right of the center a figure leans from a window holding a lamp which throws an ineluctable light upon the carnage. And over all shines the radiant eye of day, with the electric bulb of night for a pupil.[5]

I should add that the woman to the right seems to be hurling herself down on the street in flames, and that the explanation of the electric lamp as "the radiant eye of the day" is apparently conjectural and quite uncertain (fig. 1).

This description reveals at once the incongruity of the details shown. As a documentary report of an event the images assembled hardly seem to make sense. They do not add up to a naturalistic description of content, for instance, of an episode of war. They must not be read literally and objectively, like a report in a newspaper. In other words, the observer must soon become aware of the fact that the painting does not offer him simply the representation of a unified theme, as he may have been led to expect by its title; that it does not in any ordinary sense represent the destruction of a town, but something else, far more complex.

This conclusion is corroborated by the preparatory sketches which by their established sequence permit us to follow quite clearly the growth of the composition. Three stages can be distinguished. From the beginning four elements are present: the woman with the lamp, the wounded horse, the bull, and the prostrate warrior. Of these four, solely the woman with the lamp, leaning out of a window, appears at once in a pose resembling her final form (fig. 2). Only the kind of light which she is holding differs from case to case: it may be a burning candle, or a different type of lamp. On the other hand the images of the horse, the bull, and the prostrate warrior, which are likewise found in the initial sketches, undergo considerable change almost to the last. In the second stage the woman with the dead child appears near either the bull or the horse. Finally in the third

FIGURE 2. Picasso, *Guernica*, Sketch No. 1, May 1, 1937

stage emerges the present, tri-partite composition in which the bull and the woman with the dead child form a group of their own on the left. Also the two women at the right seem to have been added at this stage. The horse was placed definitely at the center. From this evidence one must conclude that precisely the comparatively realistic, illustrative items in the composition were added later, as the work progressed; while the original thought first crystallized around the elements to which a symbolic rather than direct narrative value must be ascribed, as will have to be shown presently. This original symbolic group comprises the bull, the horse, the prostrate warrior, and the woman with the lamp. Now it is certainly a point of importance here that in at least three of these figures the very reminiscences or connotations of the classical which we set out in this paper to investigate come again to the fore. A certain relation seems to exist between the symbolical functions of these images and the varying aspects of classicism which each incorporates. In the following paragraphs each shall be explored separately, yet all three must also be considered together, for their impact upon one another. As symbols they have no independent existence. As in a dream they owe their existence to one another, because they came into being by implementing each other's meaning.

We shall first concern ourselves with the woman holding a lamp. Her large head in profile and long outstretched arm, rushing across the canvas like a sudden

FIGURE 11. Ingres, *Nemesis*

FIGURE 3. Picasso, *Guernica*, detail: Woman with the lamp

FIGURE 4. Picasso, *Bullfight*, 1934, Chinese ink

gust of wind, are beautifully invented (fig 3). Together this head and arm form perhaps the most impressive detail of the entire painting, the one which we are likely to notice first and remember longest. They also constitute the first thought which assumed definite shape in the artist's own sketches, and must be regarded as one of the germinating ideas of the entire composition, much as a sequence of words suddenly occurring to a writer may in its aboriginal perfection become the nucleus of a whole poem. Yet the action of this woman, while forming a most memorable gesture, is not easily explained. Why should she wish with her poor lamp to light the street? The lamp would not avail her much on this horrible afternoon. Actually I do not think that this image represents a matter of realistic interpretation at all but draws its meaning from a different and more hidden context. For this context, we must first turn to an altogether different series of representations.

A few years before *Guernica,* in 1934, Picasso created a number of very interesting compositions dealing with bullfights. In these the bull has turned aggressor, a cruelly wounded horse is the victim. Interest focuses entirely on this group. Usually, the arena is shown rather dimly, but in some instances certain large faces in profile, apparently of women, detach themselves from the background as they bend forward to follow the scene of slaughter more closely with a mien of earnest if somewhat factual scrutiny, not unlike the tense attention with which the physicians in Rembrandt's painting follow the demonstrations of Dr. Tulp. In one case only a single onlooker, holding a burning candle, is so shown, but she seems to shy away with an expression of sudden disgust[6] (fig 4). These compositions culminate in the *Minotauromachy* of 1935, perhaps Picasso's most important etching (fig. 5). From the bull ring the scene has been transferred to a mythological setting, near a seashore and a tower. The bull has become half humanized, in the form of a Minotaur looming darkly above the doomed horse, which, curiously enough, he attacks with the sword of a *toreador*. But the onlookers have not been omitted. Two rather pretty young women observe the mythological nightmare from the window of the tower. The third is a child: a little girl. She stands near the scene of horror, which she watches intently yet without any outward signs of fear. In her raised left hand she, also, holds a burning candle. The connection between all these fantasies is obvious; so is the fact that they have a bearing on the *Guernica* mural.

We cannot here discuss the bullfight scenes in full; the bullfight, after all, is a seperate subject inviting many different thoughts. But a few remarks are in order, especially about the way in which, in these compositions, reality becomes transformed. The series starts with a live situation, the arena. It ends with a situation which seems half myth, half dream. Yet in spite of all transformations the main themes remain constant. The group of the horse and the bull renders an act of brutality committed, it appears at first, in the name of a bullfight; but it is treated eventually as a subject in its own right. This group carries many and far-reaching connotations, im-

FIGURE 5. Picasso, *Minotauromachy*, 1935, etching

plying among other characteristics a contrast of sex. It has been stated by others, and I think correctly, that in these compositions the horse is associated with feminine attributes.[7] For instance in the *Minotauromachy* the horse carries on its back the lifeless figure of a female matador. It is of course entirely possible to describe the brutal power of will as an essentially masculine, at the same time destructive, quality, and to assume that by contrast suffering is the fate of women and of the passive. This statement of the case indeed reconfirms a polarity of classical conception, built into the core of many Greek tragedies in which a comparable contrast provides the mainspring of action. To name only one instance, it certainly is not incidental that in Sophocles' drama the king, Creon, is a man, Antigone a woman. On the other hand the very realism of the tragic concept itself must warn us that no single statement of this kind can possess ultimate validity. The unwillingness to love is likely to turn into hatred at any time, with any individual. In Euripides' *Bacchae* the king becomes the slain victim and the bull-god is on the side of the frenzied women.

Be this as it may, a knowledge of Picasso's bullfight compositions provides us with a most valuable background for his *Guernica* painting. The least we can now say is that clearly these earlier compositions, which seem so fraught with private meaning, set the standard of the imagery and determined the broad scope of thought and feeling, which *Guernica* transformed into a more monumental style and a more public manifestation. We become acquainted with the interdependence of the members of the symbolic group of bull, horse, and onlooker. And we are led to recognize the same protagonists also in the *Guernica* painting, although there the bull is not visibly the aggressor and the horse was wounded by a weapon from above. True symbols have a long life and, like dreams, fit many different situations. In this sense I should say that in *Guernica,* the woman with the lamp replaces the onlooker of the former compositions. She fulfills much the same functions. Even stylistically, in the context of *Guernica,* she is an exception. If we compare her face to other details of the same painting it looks as if conceived in a different key. The reason is, obviously, that it was cast in a classical form, alien to the rest of the composition. With mouth wide open, eyes large with horror, this woman herself resembles an ancient masque of tragedy more than an ordinary, living face. Around her all creatures suffer, but hers is the only face in which, over and above the terror, we read a reaction of reason: powerless, certainly, like her useless lamp, but still expressing a certain energy of judgment, of sorrow, of outrage. The event which she witnesses is a moment of panic, turmoil beyond comprehension. Yet as an onlooker, however much involved in what she sees, as far as her stern unflinching gaze surveys the scenes of slaughter she remains a stranger to the event. She takes the part of the Chorus in a Greek tragedy, who can by the same token be described as an onlooker. It is an interesting fact that for this one face, Picasso chose the grand and, to our contemporary world, alien manner of a classic style.[8]

Yet the idea of the classic presents quite diverse facets to the modern artist, as we remarked earlier in this essay. And the other aspects of the problem have not been forgotten in the *Guernica* painting. It is one thing to discover something admirable in a classical phrase or fragment; it is another to accept the tyranny of a modern ideal, which for reasons of widely varying merit, to say the least, declares itself the classical. Artists have at all times, not only in the twentieth century, revolted against that part of the academic tradition which claims to own the models of art and the method of its production. There is nothing unusual or unjust about Picasso's often cited opinion on this, as recorded in a conversation of 1935:

Academic training in beauty is a sham. We have been deceived, but so well deceived that we can scarcely get back even a shadow of the truth. The beauties of the Parthenon, Venuses, Nymphs, Narcissuses, are so many lies. Art is not the application of a canon of beauty but what the instinct and the brain can conceive beyond any canon.[9]

Nothing could be more natural. Any artist of some creative ambition is bound to share these sentiments. At the same time they reflect the dilemma of the schools which can teach skills and perhaps, accepted tastes, but not creativity. The plaster-cast classicism of the art academies represents something more than a mere theory, at least for a young artist subject to this training. It constitutes a very real situation, and, more often than not, a problem.

One rather curious circumstance is the fact that almost

FIGURE 7. Picasso, *Studio,* 1925, oil

FIGURE 6. Picasso, *Plaster Arm,* 1893-4, pencil

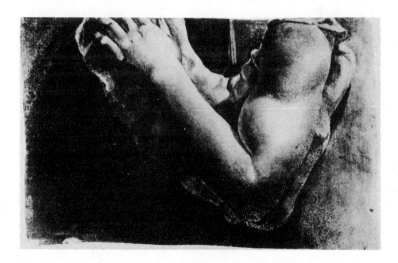

all the victims represented in the *Guernica* are women. Again in this selection the painting need not be taken literally—as if there had been no men in the town of Guernica. Rather the seemingly one-sided emphasis on the women followed quite logically from the previously established symbolism of the wounded horse which, as we have seen, with its markedly feminine overtones set the keynote also for the *Guernica* painting. There is only one obvious exception to the rule, and this quite characteristically consists in a figure which did not originally belong to the symbolic group of the horse and the Minotaur: namely, the prostrate warrior. The idea of this figure can be traced to the earlier sketches, but its form went through numerous metamorphoses. In its final shape it was reduced to three large fragments: a left arm with open palm, a head, and, severed from both, a right arm clutching a broken sword. Perhaps not without intent we are left in doubt as to whether these fragments ever belonged to a live person. They may have; but especially the arm with the sword, by way of a grim paradox, also reminds us of the academic plaster casts.

A bent arm, drawn from plaster, can be found among Picasso's earliest academic exercises from La Coruña (fig 6). Later, plaster arms appear as studio equipment occasionally combined with a sculptured head, in a series of still lifes culminating in the rather temperamental "studio" of Juan les Pins, painted during the summer of 1925 (fig. 7).[10] They now look decidedly threatening, carrying a stick or clenching their fists. But they also make us realize what strange objects they really are, torn

FIGURE 8. Picasso, *The Torso*, 1933, ink

limbs rendered harmless only by the deadly pallor of their plaster existence. To be sure, they seem to represent casts made from nature and not from sculptured models, but as household furniture of the art school and studio they easily associate with other academic, including classical, reminiscences. In a rather satirical drawing of 1933 the threatening arm, looking decidedly natural this time, is associated with the classical helmet of a warrior (fig. 8). Finally, in another drawing of the following year, in a rather hostile mood, we find the plaster arm assembled with an odd assortment of Grecian objects including a large head lying on the floor, attacked by an angry monster in the shape of a Minotaur.[11] In one of the early drawings for *Guernica,* likewise, the prostrate warrior wears a Greek helmet, thus resembling a statue toppled over rather than a real person.[12] In the final painting only the three disconnected fragments of this figure have remained. But their association with the world of the academic plaster casts can now hardly be overlooked. They look like casts, especially the head and the arm with the broken sword. Yet if indeed they carry these connotations, it also seems that they are viewed here with rather more sympathy than previously: they form so clearly a part of the epoch which perished on that fateful afternoon of spring, 1937. The arm has lost its authoritarian terror. The sword which it wielded, academic or otherwise, has proved a sadly obsolete weapon against the airplane.

After the victims, the victor. The bull has entered from the left, and now casts his cold attentive glances over the field of destruction. Obviously this bull, also, is no ordinary animal. His presence in the *Guernica* painting had been planned from the start, and the earlier sketches place him right in the center of the composition, near or above the horse. On the other hand, his form and attitude change continually in the many preliminary studies. Only one important characteristic remains constant. The head always appears more or less humanized. But even if it is entirely human, its expression and character differ from drawing to drawing. In one drawing it looks bearded, stupid, and somewhat brooding, as if its animal dullness had been translated into a human form (fig. 9). Again in another drawing it appears youthful and noble;

FIGURE 9. Picasso, *Bull's Head,* May 10, 1937, pencil

in still others, hideously monstrous.[13] In the final version
the animal form has prevailed, but in such a manner as
to leave on the face a semblance of human expression,
as of cruelty and triumph. The overall evidence thus per-
mits no doubt that the bull here is only half animal, that
to an extent he has become personified if not fully

humanized; in short, that he belongs to the large family of Picasso's Minotaurs.

The importance and frequency of the Minotaur theme in the art of Picasso between 1933 and 1937 constitutes a most remarkable fact. As a general rule mythological subjects are extremely rare in modern art after the Impressionists. Science has no room for myths. Neither did the scientific naturalism which governed the concepts of art all through the nineteenth century favor mythical fictions and imaginations. In the naturalistic school, in contrast to the academic tradition, the avoidance of subject matter not within the range of common experience was a point of principle. After the middle of the century the mythologies lost ground even in the academies. The trend of the time, which was emphatically scientific, factual, and historical, emptied the shades of the ancient myths even of that last, faint glow of life which the preceding age of reason had left in them. Their usefulness for art had ended, at least temporarily. The fact that they were not true weighed too heavily against them. The other cardinal point of the academic practice, study of the human form from life, fared better in this process. The life model could still be interpreted in terms of classical statuary, and a notion of classical form could thus survive, but hardly the classical contents. The realistic impulses in all the arts were at that time indeed the more vigorous ones, and they carried the day.

It may seem a paradoxical fact, nevertheless, that even the modernists who subsequently revolutionized the modes of seeing as well as of representation, stayed mostly within the naturalistic choice of subject matter. They may have insisted that common objects can assume quite uncommon meanings in a work of art, quite aside from the fact that art is possible without any representation at all of recognized objects. For all that, in so far as their imagery is at all concerned with reality as an objective world it mostly limited itself, and still does, to the objects at hand: the sights and experiences of indubitable existence, in a contemporary environment. As much as ever the still lifes abound, the human scene appears socially stratified, and a few traditional subjects such as the studio nude are still accepted as a pretext for the creation of a painting or a sculpture. All this, of course, is on the level of a naturalistic theory which holds art to the surface phenomena of reality. The tenor is almost Aristotelian: art deals with that which is, or which might be. Even the nameless experiences which the mind may derive from shapes visible and tangible, and which form the province of non-objective art, claim to be real on the level of immediacy. But myth is fable, and the prevailing feeling seems to be that it does not fit either Aristotelian category. It neither is, nor can it be. In the museum of modern art, mythology is rare.[14]

The Minotaur was a monster of Greek mythology, shaped as a man with a bull's head. Therefore, his every appearance, in a work of modern art, constitutes in itself a revival of an ancient symbol, regardless of whether or not the interpretation agrees with the ancient myth. Obviously the role which the Minotaur plays in the art of Picasso is a matter of considerable interest, for this special reason: it opens up a new aspect, not so far mentioned here, of the contemporary awareness of the classical. For in this instance the question is not of the merits or demerits, as the case may be, of the classical as a critical category and a mode of form, nor of the academic plaster casts and their function or lack of function in a living art. Instead the problem of the classical moves here into the focus of modern discussion by way of a third category, not as form but as content.

This observation holds for us a special interest, because in the category of content the idea of the classical underwent an even more fundamental revolution between the early nineteenth century and our own day than in the field of formal criticism. The Greek myth is not serene. It is realistic in the extreme; often it is obscure, monstrous, and revolting. Form considered by itself may be a different proposition. It is possible, though scarcely sufficient, to define classic form as a kind of decorum which brings harmonious balance to the troubled world of reality. Any such judgment depends on personal preference and the question as to where, in the long and variegated evolution of ancient art, one looks for examples. More often than not the concept, so understood, performs in the interpretation of the ancient materials a task corresponding to that which the academic tradition so often imputed to the artists: to correct nature by suppressing or eliminating that which in the natural object might offend contemporary sensibilities. Yet whatever the implications may be in modern thought, of the classic as a category of form, in the reality of ancient art these forms were at all times carriers of mythical content. And as a rule this content runs counter to a benevolent, optimistic interpretation. The Greek tragedies with all their lucid formal order do not tell pretty things. They deal with crimes, failures, and suffering; indeed with the inevitability of crime, failure, and suffering. They were the consummate expression of that realism inherent in all Greek thought. As gradually during the past two centuries more Greek literature became known and the myths were studied more perceptively, the result was inevitable. Much was unearthed from the very core of the classical heritage which could not meet the test of Olympian serenity, nor of Apollonian reason; which, by these standards, could hardly be called classical. This split within the explanations of the classical itself, caused by a more intimate knowledge and a more realistic appraisal of the classical contents, appears to have been of considerable importance for modern thought. It certainly accompanied, and even preceded, the non-academic and anti-neoclassic trends of the nineteenth-century romanticism and realism. I am inclined to assume that the early discovery of the unclassic elements in ancient daemonology or, in other words, the unclassical character of much classical lore, had its share in the formation of these trends; that is to say, of modernism.[15]

But now to return to the Minotaur and Picasso. The monster of Greek mythology lived in a dark and devious cave called the Labyrinth, on the island of Crete. Each year a group of young people was sent to him from Athens and held captive in the cave. One year the prince,

Theseus, was among them. He slew the monster and freed the captives with the help of a Cretan princess, Ariadne, who followed Theseus on his way home but was deserted by him on the island of Naxos. The story of the group of young people, the year's crop, as it were, being sent to a dark cave has anthropological parallels in other continents. On the other hand, the legend of the deserted princess who then became the bride of a god, Dionysos, seems to belong to a different, less primitive level of thought and feeling. However the fusion of these two motives into one single story may be taken as a rather typical example of the often irrational foundations, the age-old fantasies on which rested Greek intellectualism. The Greek mind remained forever sensitive to the store of symbolism which in these ancient tales stayed so peculiarly alive. Moderns were no less attracted by them whenever they realized that many truths can be expressed more fully, and certainly more compactly, in the seeming impossibilities of an ancient symbol than by discursive reason. The myth has always retained its high place in poetic content, in spite of the fact that it is conventional matter, or perhaps precisely because of that circumstance. It invites new interpretations continually. To trace the myth of Theseus, Minotaur, and Ariadne in modern letters would require a special discussion which would lead us far beyond the scope of this essay. One example is André Gide's charming paraphrase of the same story, which he turned into a perfect example of twentieth-century classicism, quietly realistic yet at the same time maintaining the quality of a lucid, indeed transparent, fable.

In 1933 Picasso drew a Minotaur for the cover of a then new magazine, entitled *Le Minotaure*.[16] It is obvious that the theme began to interest him very much. During the same year and the years immediately following, quite a few other representations of it appear in his works, mostly drawings and prints. The etching of the *Minotauromachy* was created in 1935. Soon afterward, in the years 1936 and 1937, he executed the splendid series of Minotaur compositions which still represents easily the most comprehensive, as well as the most interesting, treatment of an ancient mythical content in modern art.[17] None of these compositions tells literally a known story. On the contrary, each is a free fantasy. Yet together these fantasies form a chain of variations on a common mythical theme. We may well call them a series of *Capricci,* borrowing the term from Tiepolo and Goya. They possess the extravagance and obscure reality of dreams, and as in dreams, one thinks to perceive among the incredible happenings familiar elements: the elements of myth. There is the veiled bride, an apparition unattainable. There are moments of peril and rescue; the sea, the boat, and the departure. There is, in addition, the Minotaur. He moves through these visions as a hero of fiction moves through the passing situations of a novel. The novel in this case is a rather surrealistic one, to be sure, and he a dark hero, an infinitely threatening image composed of animal powers paired with a human will;

but while he causes terror and suffering, he also suffers. Once we see him before his cave, carrying a limp and frightened horse (fig. 10). The images of bull and Minotaur, Man-Bull and Bull-Man, have merged into one; and again the horse is the substitute victim of his violence. However, the theme is capable of variations. It happens that the horse escapes and the Amazon with it; or that in anguish, its body bursting, it becomes transformed into the benign bearded form of the rescuer raising the strong protective arm, which we also know.[18] There seems to be no end to the flow of images and their strange amalgamations. A mythical content, originally Greek, has thus been explored, and the myth found endless. Certainly the interpretations are new and arbitrary. But while the academic concepts and traditional classicism are bursting in their seams, something else instead emerges: the enduring truth, the protean life, and perhaps most important, the inherent realism of mythical symbols. This truth, this realism are always present, and their resurrection in a personal experience can happen at any time: *quod erat demonstrandum.*

When in the *Guernica* painting the Man-Bull enters, his presence remains unexplained; neither does it explain anything in the painting, expressly. Nevertheless its impact on the composition is very great. It entirely alters the tenor of meaning in the painting, revealing more clearly than any other detail the essentially symbolic, not episodic character of the latter. For now we know the violence of the bull and the blind rage of his destructive will. We have come to understand that since pure

FIGURE 10. Picasso, *Minotaur and Dying Horse*, 1936, Chinese ink and gouache

will must impose itself, its triumphs become moments of destruction. We are made to see that this is the hour when the Bull feasts on his triumph, and that he has come to survey the work completed which, as in the tragic paradox of a Greek drama, was the work of Necessity operating through human wills. The horse still is his victim. Beyond these obvious connotations, derived from the image itself and the context of Picasso's own art, I should not suggest a more definite name or denotation for the bull. Any such suggestion would be mere guesswork, and I doubt that much could be gained by it. For instance we may name this an image of war, or as Henry Kahnweiler did, of the invincible Spanish people.[19] Clearly in inventing definitions of this kind we have entered into an area where, as the road signs say, everyone travels at his own risk. The truth is that with a symbol connotations often matter more than denotations, because the same group of thought associations can fit quite diverse names and circumstances in reality. What matters first of all is the image which we see, and all possible names which one might devise can be true only as analogies of that image. They would, in the present case, only denote different instances of actuality in which the power of the Minotaur can be recognized. He himself requires no other name.

What must rather interest us is the fact itself which is beyond reasonable doubt, that a symbol of this kind, namely a mythical character in all its unmitigated strangeness, was here introduced into the representation of a real, contemporary event. Such mythical symbolism is very nearly unheard of in modern art. The symbol itself was old, of primitive, even prehistoric origin. Even the Greek Minotaur is only one of its later, mythical incorporations. Newborn children were sacrified to another, the Phoenician Moloch. One remembers the distorted figure of the mother with the dead child, so placed before the bull in the *Guernica* painting as to form almost a group with him, although the one hardly notices the other. We know of bull-masks in primitive dances, and of highly complex impersonations of the bull-god, like the Greek Dionysos, in whom the good and the perilous aspects of the creative passion have become so unaccountably united. There is, over and above the known mythological connotations, the ambiguous part which the bull plays in the severely ordered drama of the Spanish bull-games, now a hero, and then again a dark and deadly enemy.[20] The life of a symbol feeds on the associations with which we connect it, yet mutely it contains them all, as if they were so many foregone conclusions. Thus the myth must teach us that the world of primitive experience is not excluded from the classical but absorbed by it, as the living organism absorbs nourishment. It is very likely that the Man-Bull in the *Guernica* painting had Hellenic antecedents but he certainly also stems from other, less classic ancestors. This is not the only instance where by accepting mythological images into his art, Picasso seems to have discovered for himself the primitive roots of a classical content.

There remains for us to say a word about style. In a work of art, style and meaning affect each other mutually; they are inseparable. In the *Guernica* painting, also, the use of symbolic imagery is a matter of style as much as of content. It is equally unusual on either level, if compared to the prevailing habits of modern art where even symbolism is likely to be expressed in common and natural rather than mythical images. The formal composition of the painting itself is very interesting. It is oblong yet centered, as are many monumental compositions of ancient art. Thus even the formal order carries classical overtones, and produces comparable results. The effect is a certain static monumentality seemingly in contradiction to the vehement movements in which it becomes established, thereby creating a strong feeling of formal tension. Needless to say, with Picasso, any reference to other art or a certain manner of style, no less than references to nature, must undergo radical formal transformations. For the creation of images at which his art is aiming is not compatible with copying, nor is the creation of a picture the same as "composition." Yet from the severe isolation of forms and fragments of forms, which characterizes this style, and from the transformations which permit these shapes to enter into a purely compositional context, the images draw their peculiar strength. Their test of truth is the degree to which they become memorable. The symbolic selection of the images, suggesting possible rather than representing actual meanings, enhances this effect. One may doubt if any more episodic approach, in the manner of a journalistic report, could have served the purpose as well. It is remarkable how many elements which one might deem essential have been omitted from this representation. Not a single airplane appears in it. Indeed the electric street lamp in its unrelieved bareness is the most modern thing in the entire painting. Obviously the mechanics of the destruction do not matter here, only their human causes. Yet it is precisely this transforming selection that lifts the accident from the plane of an episodic record of a deplorable event to the level of thought where the event reveals another, paradigmatic meaning. No more common imagery could have given the same effect of concise monumentality. The *Guernica* painting by Picasso is not only an artistic reflection on a given subject matter. It is also a reflection on art itself.

NOTES

1 The design room in the Art School of San Telmo, Malaga, offers a typical example: R. Penrose, *Portrait of Picasso* (New York, 1957), p. 11, fig. 4. The collection includes casts of ancient heads and statues—one recognizes the Apollo of the Palazzo Vecchio in the rear—but also statuette-replicas, among them the Venus of Milo. Notice in addition the small replica of Michelangelo's *Night*. It may be worth mentioning here that in 1919 Picasso drew a reclining nude, obviously from another of Michelangelo's Medici statues, the *Dawn:* Chr. Zervos, *Pablo Picasso* (Paris, 1949), III, pl. 104, fig. 296. Variations: *Ibid.*, III, pl. 130, fig. 388, and VI (1954), pl. 163, figs. 1369, 1370; in the last named drawing the Michelangelesque overtones, still noticeable, include reminiscences of the *Night*, as well. Cf. *Bather* of the same year, *Ibid.*, III, pl. 119, fig. 358.

2 Female arm, ca. 1893-1894, and other studies of casts from nature: Chr. Zervos, *Dessins de Picasso* (Paris, 1949), pl. 4; Zervos, *Pablo Picasso*, VI, pl. 1, figs. 5-8. Casts of ancient sculpture: male torso, *Ibid.*, VI, fig. 1; so-called *Theseus*, Parthenon East, *Ibid.*, VI, fig. 4; so-called *Kephissos*, Parthenon West, *Ibid.*, VI, pl. 16, fig. 125. The latter drawing is listed by Zervos as dating from Barcelona, 1897.

3 Picasso's neoclassic style was more extensively discussed in the preceding essay, pp. 90 ff. Its manifestations begin to appear around 1917; witness the drawing of a female head, Zervos, *Pablo Picasso*, III, pl. 26, fig. 77 (after a Greek red-figured vase or a reproduction?). This particular phase lasted till ca. 1923, according to A. H. Barr, Jr., *Picasso: Fifty Years of His Art* (New York, 1946), pp. 115 ff. Cf. F. Elgar and R. Maillard, *Picasso* (New York, 1956), especially pp. 88 ff., 117 ff.; other bibliography in the following footnotes. The neoclassic significance of outline drawing was discussed by D. and E. Panofsky, *Pandora's Box* (New York, 1956), pp. 90 ff.

4 Data on the history of the painting can be found in A. H. Barr, Jr., *Picasso: Fifty Years of His Art*, pp. 195 ff.; J. Larrea, *Guernica: Pablo Picasso* (New York, 1947). The latter publication includes a highly informative sequence of preparatory sketches dating from May 1 to the middle of June, 1937; figs. 34-78. Cf. in addition the illustrated catalogue, *Guernica* (Brussels, 1956), and the similar, well-documented catalogue later published in Stockholm where the same exhibition moved subsequently: *Guernica,* Preface by C. Sköld (Stockholm, 1956); for the latter information my thanks go to Axel Boethius. Composition and interpretation: J. Runnquist, *Minotauros: En Studie i förhållandent mellan Ikonografi och Form i Picassos Konst 1900-1937* (Stockholm, 1959), pp. 136 ff.; W. Boeck and J. Sabartès, *Picasso* (New York, 1955), pp. 225 ff.; also P. Wescher, "Picasso's Guernica and the Exchangeability of the Picture Parts," *Art Quarterly*, XVIII (1955), pp. 346 ff. It must be pointed out, however, that contrary to Wescher, *op. cit.*, p. 346, the woman leaning out of the window does *not* hold a candle but an old-

fashioned oil lamp; nor can this lamp be considered an effective source of light in the painting, for the reasons stated above.

5 A. H. Barr, Jr., *Picasso: Fifty Years of his Art*, p. 200.

6 Chr. Zervos, *Dessins de Picasso*, pl. 84, fig. 118. Zervos, *Pablo Picasso* (Paris, 1957) VIII, pl. 99, fig. 215; July 24, 1934. Cf. *Ibid.*, VIII, pl. 98, fig. 212.

7 D. E. Schneider, "The Painting of Pablo Picasso: A Psychoanalytic Study," *College Art Journal*, VII (1947-48), pp. 86 ff.

8 "Classic," in this case, does not necessarily mean "Greek." It appears that the woman with the lamp in the *Guernica* painting has her antecedents primarily in French neoclassic art; especially the figure of Nemesis in Ingres' *L'apothéose de Napoléon Ier*, and preparatory sketches, for which see A. Mongan, *Drawings from the Collection of Curtis O. Baer* (Cambridge, Mass., 1958), pp. 53 ff., No. 43. In this connection it is interesting to note that F. Elgar calls Picasso's figure itself a "Nemesis": F. Elgar and R. Maillard, *Picasso* (New York, 1956), p. 170. (fig. 11.)

9 A. H. Barr, Jr., *Picasso: Fifty Years of His Art*, p. 273.

10 See note 2. Another, very monumental if rather spastic, specimen of the painted plaster arm, also dated 1925, is included in *Picasso: An American Tribute* (New York, 1962), "Paul Rosenberg and Co., The Twenties," fig. 39.

11 Chr. Zervos, *Dessins de Picasso*, pl. 81, fig. 114.

12 J. Larrea, *Guernica: Pablo Picasso*, fig. 41.

13 *Ibid.*, figs. 55, 61. May 11th and 20th, 1937.

14 Exceptions can of course be found. For instance, important representations of the Prometheus theme occur both in the art of Lipchitz and Orozco: cf. H. R. Hope, *The Sculpture of Jacques Lipchitz* (New York, 1954), pp. 16 ff.; D. W. Scott, "Orozco's Prometheus," *College Art Journal*, XVII (1957), pp. 2 ff.

15 It can be shown that a sharp decline of classical erudition set in after 1600, compared to the previous high Renaissance level; G. Bagnani, "Winckelmann and the Second Renascence, 1755-1955," *American Journal of Archaeology*, LIX

(1955), pp. 107 ff. Yet during the same period the collecting of ancient art—casts and originals alike—was on the rise. Especially the fashionable art collections in Holland deserve more attention in this respect than was so far accorded to them. They shed much light on Baroque and late-Baroque classicism, outside the just then diminishing range of literary scholarship: the classicism of the *dilettanti, virtuosi,* noblemen, and academies. Characteristically, the "Second Renascence" turned to the critique of art (Winckelmann) and letters (Bentley) with equal energy. At the same time it imposed a new rule of scholarship, i.e., historicism, on either discipline. The ensuing uncertainty regarding the moral and esthetic evaluation of antiquity—or in other words, the meaning of the word classical—may therefore well be called a result of modern historical criticism, the first consequences of which became apparent shortly after 1800. Such criticism is in itself a demonstration of realism; and when, as was then the case, it combines with a feeling of admiration for the objects investigated, it indeed deserves the name of a romantic realism. In this appraisal I also find myself in agreement with J. Barzun, *Romanticism and the Modern Ego* (Boston, 1947), pp. 273 ff. It must therefore seem a remarkable fact that this romantic, historical modernism first established itself in a critique of "classical" antiquity; and that one of its first fruits was a "re-evaluation of values" in this obviously crucial field, pursued in open contrast to the normative, practical rather than speculative usage of *classical* in the traditional academic sense. See also above, pp. 85 ff. and for details, regarding the transformation of *la belle antiquité* into a new concept of antiquity which deliberately included the dark forces of "chthonic" and "dionysiac" religion, G. Highet, *The Classical Tradition* (Oxford, 1951), pp. 466 ff.; W. Müri, *Die Antike: Untersuchung über den Ursprung und die Entwicklung der Bezeichnung einer geschichtlichen Epoche* (Bern, 1957).

16 Illustrated in A. H. Barr, Jr., *Picasso: 75th Anniversary Exhibition* (New York, 1957), p. 93.

17 Frequently illustrated. See especially Chr. Zervos, *Dessins de Picasso*, figs. 121, 123, 125; Zervos, *Pablo Picasso*, VIII, pls. 135 ff., fig. 285-288. F. Elgar and R. Maillard, *Picasso*, p. 178, color reproduction of *Minotaur and Dying Horse;* p. 185, *Blind Minotaur*. A thoughtful account of the entire series is included with J. Runnquist, *Minotauros*, pp. 118 ff.; cf. above, note 4. A parallel in contemporary English letters, the Minotaur symbol introduced by way of a dream, may be quoted from *The Collected Poetry of W. H. Auden* (New York, 1954), pp. 209 ff.

> And a bull with the face of the Vicar
> Was charging with lowered horn.

18 Chr. Zervos, *Dessins de Picasso*, fig. 125.

19 Introduction to *Guernica* (Brussels, 1956); reprinted in subsequent catalogues of the same exhibition, cf. note 4. See also *Picasso: Peintures 1900-1955* (Paris, 1955), text to no. 87, *Guernica;* W. Boeck and J. Sabartès, *Picasso*, pp. 230 ff.; V. Marrero, *Picasso and the Bull* (Chicago, 1956), especially pp. 57 ff., 75 ff.

20 Cf. V. Marrero, *op. cit.*, pp. 32 ff.

Standing Woman, Greek,
III cent., B.C., terra cotta
(7½" high)

Braque, *Femme Debout*, 1920,
plaster (7¾″ high)

Stephen Greene

"CURSED BE that mortal inter-debtedness . . . I would be as free as air," says Herman Melville, and twentieth-century painting echoes that cry—most particularly to that influence, direct or indirect, that remains of classical art. For more than five hundred years painting owed a "mortal inter-debtedness" to the Greek tradition as it was "rediscovered" and revitalized by the Renaissance, so that today we find ourselves repudiating the one with the other.

Unless we happen to be a Picasso—in which case we may use our freedom to employ the material of other art epochs, including the classical, to create new forms and new meanings—our works do not reflect the classics. However, genius such as that of Picasso cannot be fitted to the measure of a particular time and his use of classical forms and myths is an aspect of his art and not the core of it; nor is it the core of our particular *zeitgeist*. Rather, our time has found sympathy with the art of Negro fetiches, childlike and ominous visions, the art of primitive peoples, totally anti-classical in spirit and necessity. Painters do not fix their eyes on perfect truth as a perpetual standard of reference nor do we deal with canons of "things beautiful."

Likewise the naturalistic aspect of classical art has virtually disappeared. It is a different sense of proportion and order that now imposes itself upon us. What, according to the Greek mode, would have been considered disproportion and disorder now underlie our images. We do not commence with a unity which is ideal or express ourselves in terms of concrete experience. We begin with the fragment, and the importance of fragmentation is not lost when the work is completed. The concept of the classical style as "idealistic" and of classical art as representing a better world of ethically and aesthetically superior beings is foreign to us. Actually all that remain are certain classical modes as can be observed in the "order," the "ideal unity" of a Mondrian, the well-modulated formality of a Braque, and the serene repose of a Matisse.

The most important aspect of Greek art to my work has not been the classical iconography—sculpture and drawings—but what exists in Greek drama: the tragic sense. Tragedy always seems to assume the fundamental dignity and worth of man. The philosophical problem of the worth of life continues to be a dominant theme of art in the twentieth century. This could not have come into existence without our self-consciousness, self-observation, and self-criticism, which are the part of Western culture that derives from the Greek tradition. Antigone knows from the outset that she must die for the act of burying her brother's corpse. This examination of the life-death, suicide theme—Haemon and Eurydice, as well as Antigone take their lives—this necessity for self-destruction at the ebb of life's worth powerfully restates the value of life.

The painters of our time who are concerned with the tragic sense work under certain disadvantages. Ours is a nonreligious age. Greek art was primarily religious in character. The gods could be reached through an image representing them, the image of man. A Picasso *Crucifixion* has its own magic, a formal meaning with limited religious connotations. My own work makes use of the religious theme to clarify a contemporary sense of life but it is not based on religious belief. Rouault is a religious man and a religious painter but the appreciation of his work comes mainly from secular quarters.

There is no religion without at least one figure of high station. Today, we are interested in the fall of Everyman rather than in the fall of figures of high station. We no longer believe that fate like an unknown, outside force strikes us. We have begun to know wherein lie our own responsibilities for our fatal flaws. Oedipus unknowingly kills his father, marries his mother. Perhaps it is a profounder truth and equally moving that not "fate" but we ourselves have led to our own crimes and our responsibility for them is therefore greater. With "fate," the hero or figure of high station, as well as the image of man practically destroyed, what remains of the tragic sense in twentieth-century art? The new myth lies in the fragments of Everyman's existence, the fragments of his imagination, his irrationality, his unconscious, his violence, and his absurdity . . . with or without his image. Democracy has enlarged the importance of each individual, even when he is half-lost in the confusion of existence. We have finally replaced the heroes of the past and taken the stage ourselves.

Our tragic sense derives from a sense of man with or without his image. This can be seen directly in Picasso's *Dreams and Lies of Franco,* in *Guernica,* and in a number of his still lifes of the forties; also in the compassionate configuration of Rouault; in the haunted, elongated figures of Giacometti; occasionally in the brooding, swift, black lines of Franz Kline; and in the overpowering force, like a cataclysmic agent, of De Kooning's abstractions. In the work of Max Beckmann, the figures take their places like formalized, strong but doomed characters in a play. In my own work, the tragic sense informs the entire image and Everyman, so that in a Flagellation it is not only the Christ figure that suffers but also his torturers. We are all involved, we are all responsible.

Our century has known Cubism, Dadaism, Futurism,

Vorticism, Surrealism—movements neither classical nor tragic. As art has become more and more the discovery of self, of automatism, of the non-preordained picture, the possibilities of the world of painting have become more and more diversified. The range of painting is no longer narrowly confined, it now embraces the whole wide range of the human personality.

Many of the gifted younger painters work solely with abstract forms. A successful abstract painting conjures up a world, not one seen but a felt experience that at times can convey a concept of tragedy. Jackson Pollock's work has the Dionysian faculty of rejoicing and suffering in the exaltation of the instincts. In his last paintings there is a majestic and doomed rush of line, a possible sense of the tragic. If I find his work not successful, it is because of the preponderance of the maze-like structure, his lack of the forceful clarity of forms and ideas necessary to a great artist. Pollock was a tragic figure and the emotive force of his personality and originality came through in his work. Whether the tragic sense in American painting has yet matured is doubtful, but what is certain is that a number of important painters are concerned with this problem.

Many painters have turned away from the image of man. This separation implies a statement on man's condition. It took more than the advent of the camera, Freud, and Cubism to diminish the importance of the image of man in painting. Nor is it a question of outmoded, threadbare realism or naturalism. These can no longer be tolerated and even a created image of man is more than most painters today can bear. This is in part due to the removal of the concept of the hero; we question God and immortality, and our motives are increasingly suspect. The Greeks gave us our heroes, Christianity, our saints, and we have given ourselves, ourselves.

Classical Greek art was poised and balanced, unmystical; our art is mystical, often unpoised, and willing to face our unbalance. It is now harder to believe in man and therefore to believe in his image as created. Destruction is nothing new but certainly we are more adept at it, witness the German gas chambers and Hiroshima. We know man's petty daily acts, his viciousness and ineffectiveness. We are aware of the inner convolutions that lie behind the outer image. Man, who is also capable of the love of life and the good acts of life, falls into disgrace when he faces himself and, dying, is robbed of immortality. This is the fall of man. Our high estate is our possibilities which we tragically cannot fulfill.

An artist is not like other people in his concern with making out of the truths he has found an artifice, his work. But an artist as a man can hope that life should not be something to just endure but something worth enduring. We do question ourselves and create new systems of value and as we do so, our indebtedness to the Greek heritage is revealed, the heritage that has been the base for a concept of tragedy and a renewed sense of the worth of life.

Draped Female Torso,
Roman, II cent. A.D., marble

Roger Sessions

I F WE LOOK for direct influences of Greek or Roman music on the music of the Middle Ages, Renaissance, and the nineteenth and twentieth centuries, we find only two; these two influences, however, are fundamental ones.

First of all, we owe our scale system to the Greeks; or to put it differently, the Greeks organized tones for us. They laid the basis for the whole system of tones on which the music of Western civilization depends. It is true that medieval musical theory—the direct ancestor of our own—actually derives from a mistranslation of Greek texts. To the Greeks, the concepts "high" and "low" meant the opposite of what the terms mean to us;

the result is that, while we customarily begin our scales on the lowest tone and carry them upward, the Greeks began theirs on what we would consider the highest tone and carried them downward. This misunderstanding, which arose in the very early Middle Ages, resulted, however, in a distortion of the theoretical framework rather than of actual results. Our scale system still has its foundations in the musical ideas of the Greeks.

Music and the scale system on which it is based, has of course developed and changed very considerably in the last two thousand years. Musicians have discovered possibilities inherent in it which, from all evidence at hand, were not only unknown but undreamed-of by the Greeks, either in theory or in practice. Any evidence that the Greeks explored the effects obtainable by singing or playing two or more tones together at any interval other than the octave is dubious, or at best highly controversial. What we call polyphony or counterpoint, and harmony—at least in the narrow sense of the word—were therefore unknown to them. Harmony, in the broader sense of relationships between tones, however, was a part of the Greek musical tradition; in fact, here lies our basic debt to the Greeks. For, out of an awareness that such harmonic relationships exist and the effort to understand them, the Greek scale-system, and consequently our own, was developed. We may also assume that the Greeks carried it to the farthest degree of refinement possible at the time. It is entirely likely, however undemonstrable (I believe that such propositions are undemonstrable by their very nature), that further development of the scale-system was bound to wait on the discovery and development of polyphonic, and later of harmonic, principles in order to take place on any but an entirely arbitrary basis.

In any case, the organization of musical tone as Western culture has adopted it, has remained in all essentials unchanged. If the implications of the tonal system for us today—and for several previous centuries—are in certain respects radically different from those which the system held for the Greeks, this is due to the evolution of the musical idiom and not to any departure which could be conceived as a repudiation of this heritage. The essential materials remain the same. We use the same twelve tones postulated by their system and, at least thus far, no others.

The only other direct influence of classical culture on our music is, it seems to me, in the development of opera. The musicians who met at the Palazzo Bardi in Florence toward the end of the sixteenth century and produced the first essays in the form we now know as opera, had actually the intention of providing Greek, or more properly speaking, Classical drama. Not only were the texts of the early operas taken in the main, if not exclusively, from classical myth or history (witness the titles *Euridice, Dafne, Orfeo,* and later *La Corazione di Poppea,* and *Arianna*), but above all, opera was conceived as a revival of the classical *form* of drama. Some of its devices —most obviously, of course, the chorus—show very clear traces of this derivation. That opera has developed along its own and quite different lines does not lessen the significance of its origin in the impact of classical culture on the Renaissance. Opera has, of course, been subject to all the influences prevalent in Western culture as a whole. Not only has opera followed lines determined by our cultural environment, but the varieties of treatment that the art has developed—far wider in range than might appear at first glance—have been strongly conditioned by individual factors, which result from the fact that opera is the most elaborate, complex, and even expensive art form. This fact has bound it even more closely to the exigencies of time and place than either music or drama have been and has given rise to a wide variety of solutions to the basic problem of opera, that is, the combining of several arts.

For the Greeks themselves this problem presumably did not exist. The evolution of Greek drama seems to present a relatively orderly and straightforward aspect; nowhere does one receive the impression that the combination of poetical, dramatic, and musical elements was a problem in their eyes. On the other hand, the problem of combining arts lies at the very core of the operatic situation. This is true precisely because opera was conceived as a revival of ancient art forms—forms which, after the Classical period, had an independent existence and separate growth. These forms thus had developed claims of their own. Not only did these separate and at times even disparate claims have to be reconciled, but the arts had to come together under varying conditions of language, tradition, and economic and social structure, resulting in a wide variety of forms. Yet in the history of operatic development the source-image of opera as the inheritor of a Greek dramatic idea keeps recurring, and though opera presents itself under the widest possible variety of aspects, it is doubtful whether its ancient predecessor has ever been completely lost from view.

We cannot come closer than these two fundamentals —opera and scale system—to a genuinely direct influence of classical antiquity on our music. We know a great deal about Greek, and by implication, Roman, music and especially about Greek musical theory. We do not, however, know with any certainty what Greek music sounded like. Some of us have tried to guess, and it is quite likely that certain fragments have been reconstructed with accuracy as far as the actual notes are concerned. There is too much, however, that we do not really know. We can only guess at how these notes sounded in performance; such matters as rhythm—aside from what we can learn from the prosody of Greek poetry—tempo and dynamic expression remain matters on which we can merely speculate. Still more important, we do not really know—and it is by the very nature of the situation impossible to know—what music meant, in terms of expressive content, to the Greeks. A clear example of our helplessness may be seen if we try to interpret Plato's meaning when he condemned music written in the Lydian mode—corresponding in external form to our scale in C-major—as debilitating, and endorsed the Dorian mode—corresponding roughly to our scale of E-minor—as apt to inculcate or promote the manly virtues.

Aside, therefore, from scale system and opera, the influence of classical tradition on music is found in reflections of Greek or Roman culture in general. They are, in fact, influences not upon music itself, but upon ideas or words in association with music. I have already referred to the preponderance of "classical" themes in the texts of the very earliest operas. This prevalence lasted in fact well into the eighteenth century. Let us note in passing what is for us the most celebrated opera of the middle or late seventeenth century, the *Dido and Aeneas* of Henry Purcell. Moving into the eighteenth century, we find very much the same type of influence. The operas of Handel and of his contemporary Rameau are to a large extent classical in theme, although in the case of Rameau one may legitimately raise the question whether antiquity did not arrive indirectly by way of French seventeenth century tragedy. The classical element here derives from a general cultural influence, prevalent especially in the Latin countries, rather than a specific effect on music. Gluck's operas reflect a similar influence. Of his most celebrated works, only the *Armide* has a source which is not derived from Greek myth. In the latter part of the century, as German opera began to develop, classical subjects occurred less frequently, though we find traces in the work of Mozart (*Idomeneo* and *Titus*) and even Beethoven in his rather remotely "classical" ballet, *The Men of Prometheus*. If we stretch the point still further, we may include even Schubert, to whom quasi-classical themes came only incidentally, by way of Goethe and Schiller.

Throughout the nineteenth century, in fact, classical influence even on this level remains slight, sporadic, and even problematical. It is for the most part confined to opera, and in most cases it is a matter of décor. Bellini's *Norma*, for instance, is a thoroughly romantic love story and the fact that the opera setting happens to be in Britain under the Roman conquest is of no substantial significance; the opera's action could easily be in a number of other places. Spontini's *La Vestale* belongs to a certain degree in the same category, while the *Medea* of Cherubini is clearly of more authentically classical nature. The same may be said, of course, of Berlioz' *Les Troyens*, consisting of *The Capture of Troy* in three acts and *The Trojans in Carthage* in five. For the sake of completeness one should add, no doubt, Massenet's Gallicized and decidedly *fin de siècle*, *Phèdre*, although here again the question of actual classical influence becomes tenuous. Two symphonic poems of Liszt, *Orpheus* and *Prometheus*, might also be included; the *Prometheus*, however, is based on Hender.

The twentieth-century musical picture is different; although complex, the classical influence is clearer than in the previous century. Let us note first the names of a few of the best known works which suggest Greek influence: *The Afternoon of a Faun* by Debussy, *Daphnis and Chloe* by Ravel, *Elektra* by Strauss; of a more recent generation, *Oedipus Rex*, *Apollon Musagète*, *Persephone*, *Orpheus*, and most recently *Agon* by Stravinsky; of a still younger generation, *Oresteia* of Milhaud, *Antigone* of Honegger, Krenek's *Orpheus*, *Orestes*, and *Medea*, the

Carmina Burana and *The Triumph of Aphrodite* by Orff, the ballet *Marsyas*, *Songs* from the Greek anthology, poems of Anacreon; and the very recent *Cinque Canti* of Dallapicola. Although the prevalence of classical themes is possibly greatest among the French composers, it is not confined to one school or trend in contemporary music; virtually all are represented, with the possible exception of the extremely important Viennese group. Even this group, in fact, is perhaps represented by a work, now virtually forgotten, which enjoyed some success for a few years—the opera *Die Bacchantinnen* by Egon Wellesz.

In the United States we have made less use of the classical themes; but I might add to my list my own *Idyll of Theocritus*, and possibly my opera, *The Trial of Lucullus*. Among the younger composers, the *Medea* ballet of Samuel Barber, the *Minotaur* and the music for the *Philoctetes* of Sophocles by Elliot Carter may be mentioned. More recent works are a very striking set of choruses from Sophocles by Seymour Shifrin and a cantata, *The Lament of Hecuba*, by William Carlin.

I have not even mentioned Eric Satie's *Socrate*, or Gabriel Fauré's *Penelope*, works by two composers who perhaps belong to the end of the nineteenth century rather than to the twentieth century; and the list is still not complete.

What all these musical works suggest is the great variety, and also an inventiveness of conception, characteristic of twentieth-century music in general. In the twentieth century, the classical tradition obviously has many different meanings to a variety of composers. In some compositions it seems to be a question simply of a certain exotic coloring, for instance in Debussy's *The Afternoon of a Faun* and even Ravel's *Daphnis and Chloe*. Others such as Carl Orff seem to be attracted to the pagan eroticism, in this case definitely vulgarized. Still other composers have been deeply affected by the dark and irrational elements in Greek mythology; possibly the *Elektra* of Strauss is the most celebrated example. In a third category are the pseudo or neoclassicism of Satie and Fauré in the works previously mentioned, and the monumental remoteness of Stravinsky's *Oedipus Rex*, a remoteness which the composer has underlined by his use of a Latin text—a Latin which is, I believe, legal or ecclesiastical rather than classical. We may in fact by way of summary make a rough classification on the basis of the works cited above:

FIRST. Direct settings of classical texts, usually in translation. The *Socrate* of Eric Satie is a setting of passages from Plato narrating the story of the death of Socrates. Others include Dallapiccola's three song cycles, Orff's settings of Catullus, the *Philotetes* by Carter, the Sophoclean choruses of Shifrin, and my own setting of Trevelyan's translation of the *Second Idyll* of Theocritus.

SECOND. Works based on more or less free adaptations of Greek tragedy, such as the *Oresteia* of Milhaud, the *Antigone* of Honegger, the *Oedipus Rex* of Stravinsky, the *Orestes* of Krenek, and in a more problematical sense the *Elektra* of Strauss.

It is worth mentioning that these two categories are essentially characteristic of the twentieth century; with very slight qualification one can certainly say that nothing quite as frankly and literally taken from classical literature has played so important a role in the music of any previous period.

> THIRD. Works based on classical subjects and supposedly embodying in some degree an aspect of the classical spirit. Besides those works already mentioned are the two operas of Strauss, which are perhaps of lesser importance and certainly lesser artistic merit, *The Egyptian Helen* and *The Loves of Danaë*. Also in this category may be found works with classical connections which are, as it were, incidental. A convenient example is my own opera, *The Trial of Lucullus*. The subject is the trial of an illustrious conqueror after his death, before a jury of common people, to determine whether he shall be sent for eternity to Hades or to the Elysian Fields. The text is a radio play by Bertholt Brecht, written for the Zurich radio at the time of Hitler's invasion of Poland. The setting is of course Roman, both above and below the ground, but it is clear that Rome has here the significance of an all-powerful imperial symbol, and that the classical tradition does not in any real sense enter into the play.

It is obvious that composers, like other artists of today, are very much aware of the heritage that remains from classical antiquity, and have responded in many ways to its varied fascinations. To be sure, it is most unlikely that a future age will consider all the works cited as important; some of them will be forgotten. Nevertheless, taken together, they do constitute a noteworthy portion of the musical production of our time, and can be considered as indicating a genuinely characteristic trend.

My own conviction is that opera is undergoing another transformation. Several of the most important works of recent years—by no means all of them based on strictly classical subjects—seem to me to indicate the emergence of a type of opera which will be concerned directly with the most profound of human ideas. In these operas the dramatic action will be condensed and summary, and the over-all design will find its motivation more outspokenly in musical—as opposed to literary—exigencies than has often been the case in the past. This is not the place to attempt a precise definition of the tendency which I have in mind, nor is the time ripe for such definition. Yet a number of works already exist, of undeniable dramatic power, in which the action is concentrated to a degree unthinkable on the purely literary stage; the dramatic core of these operas is embodied in a basic design and convention which derives even more strongly from the specifically musical conception than from the literary one. This, of course, has always in a sense been true of opera at its most felicitous. But such works as the *Wozzeck* of Alban Berg, the *Oedipus Rex* of Stravinsky, and perhaps above all the *Moses and Aaron* of Schoenberg—and there are others—seem to me in their several manners to point the way to new possibilities, perhaps even themselves to embody these possibilities. The widespread contemporary treatment of classical themes and the highly concentrated and often almost stylized manner in which they are treated seems to me to be one more, even though a relatively less obvious, indication of the development of this tendency toward reducing the story to its essential elements and thus giving to the music the greatest possible scope in development of its expressive potentialities. To me at least, it is not far-fetched to regard this, too, as ultimately derived from an intimation of the Greek spirit, which continues to reappear in various manifestations at critical moments in the development of the arts.

In any case, it is clear that in music, as in other aspects of our present-day cultural world, the classical tradition is very much alive. Possibly the very variety and richness of its manifestations are an indication of its vitality in a world beset by problems both frightening and unprecendented.

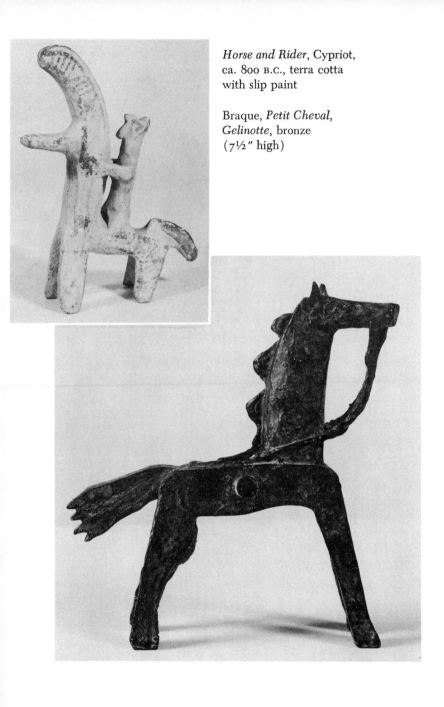

Horse and Rider, Cypriot,
ca. 800 B.C., terra cotta
with slip paint

Braque, *Petit Cheval,
Gelinotte*, bronze
(7½" high)

Herbert J. Muller

MY SUBJECT, I must confess a little wearily, involves the old, old story of the glory that was Greece and the grandeur that was Rome. I have gone through this story three times now, in different books, and each time have come out with the same commonplace conclusion, of the supreme importance of the Greeks in particular, and our immense indebtedness to them. It seems obvious to me that life as we know it began with the Greeks, and that even the very different kind of life we have gone on to make for ourselves is an outgrowth of the spirit that entered history with them.

Yet this is not really obvious. Most Americans are

hardly aware of all that we owe to the Greeks; for them the classical tradition is as dead as the classical languages, or as meaningless as the classical columns stuck on many county courthouses. Moreover, my subject involves a controversial issue, a kind banned on American air waves. I am told that we are now officially a nation under God—a God unknown to the ancient Greeks. Many thinkers are asserting that our Christian religion was the fountainhead of our ideals of freedom and democracy, and insisting that only on a Christian basis can we hope to preserve these ideals. They will admit that classical culture played a very important part in shaping Christianity, but most stress its essential difference from Christianity. Certainly the historic Jesus of the synoptic Gospels was not steeped in classical culture, and seemed wholly indifferent to it. St. Paul, the Apostle to the Gentiles, flatly rejected the wisdom of the Greeks as mere foolishness or sinful pride. Paul in particular forces this issue by his insistence that there was no real virtue or hope for man except through Christ. It may seem merely academic to worry over the question of just where the Western ideals of freedom came from, since they are here anyway; but the question involves basic differences in belief and spirit that are not at all academic if we hope that these ideals are here to stay.

Now I should say at once that I see no necessity for declaring that either the classical or the Christian tradition was *the* fountainhead of our freedoms. I make out various historical sources. Christianity seems to me clearly a major one, especially through its principles of

spiritual equality, the brotherhood of man, the dignity
and worth of the individual—phrases that may sound
pretty hollow these days, but that I believe still have
some real meaning and force, and must have if we are to
have any hope of saving our kind of society. Another
primary source was the rise of the middle class, beginning in the free towns of the Middle Ages; for quite un-
ideal reasons, the busy bourgeois were a major factor
in the growth and spread of freedom. Among other in-
digenous factors was the growth of parliamentary institutions—institutions virtually unknown in the ancient
world. None of these various factors can be measured
or weighed. I think we have no logical right to speak of
the "real" or the "ultimate" cause of historical developments—as if the invisible connections that we somehow
make out, and designate as "causes," were plainly
stamped with some quality of superior realness or ulti-
macy. But since historians still do talk this way, I should
argue that the classical legacy is as important as any
other source of our freedom, and that it may well be the
deepest source, as it is certainly the oldest one.

This much seems clear. The Greeks developed the
conscious ideal of freedom long before Christianity,
without benefit of clergy; democracy at least got started
on a non-religious basis. Medieval society—the heyday
of Christianity—was not a free or democratic society.
The major established churches did not then lead the
movement toward freedom, but typically were hostile
to it; the secular Age of Enlightenment provided the
main impetus. Hence the distinguished Catholic philos-

opher Jacques Maritain, who believes that a truly Christian society should be democratic, has confessed that God worked in mysterious ways, choosing to reveal through free thinkers and unbelievers the political implications of Christianity, to which the leaders of His Church had been blind for many centuries. In these terms, my thesis is that God worked His will by reviving the classical tradition, or more broadly the Greek spirit; while also inspiring Christian businessmen with enterprise, or what His ministers called greed, and later putting heretical ideas into the heads of Protestants, causing a bloody religious conflict that finally led to the ideal of religious freedom or freedom of conscience.

My subject is accordingly a very large one. It is still larger because to appreciate the influence of classical culture one needs a broad conception of freedom, embracing not only political but intellectual freedom, freedom of mind and spirit, the power and the desire to choose and carry out one's own purposes, the basic attitudes and habits of thought essential to the functioning of a free society. Likewise one needs to take a broad view of classical culture, embracing much more than the academic classical tradition, which was generally aristocratic, conservative, bookish, and remote from the spirit of Greece in its prime. In this view "influences" become more pervasive and indirect, still harder to specify with any precision or assurance. Needless to say, I cannot cover so much ground at all adequately in this short essay, and am bound to simplify as I gallop through the centuries; but on the assumption that there is never any serious danger of disarming criticism, I shall touch on three main topics: first, the nature of the classical legacy; then the actuality of its influence; and lastly the basic issues it raises. For what seem to me the most valuable ideas that have come out of it are all debatable (a nice academic word for "controversial").

I take for my text the parable of the Grand Inquisitor in Dostoyevsky's *Brothers Karamazov:* the Inquisitor who recognized the true Christ, returned to earth, but nevertheless sentenced him to death again. Christ, he said, was offering men spiritual freedom—and for the great masses of men such freedom is an intolerable burden. What they need first of all is bread, and then "miracle, mystery, authority." "Man seeks not so much God as the miraculous." Freedom appals man, Santayana added: "he is afraid of a universe that leaves him alone." Now man in the early civilizations of the East was certainly a slave to such needs, and such fears. In ancient Egypt, Mesopotamia, and India alike his whole culture was based on religion. His religion was no more spiritual, to be sure, than popular religion is today; what he sought from the gods was not holiness but good crops, health, virility, success in war, a prodigiously long life. The difference was that he really depended on the gods to produce these worldly goods, and in return he had to serve the gods and their priests; although he might complain when the gods fell down on their job, he hardly dreamed of spiritual freedom.

Obedience to authority was likewise the ruling principle in his social and political life. The characteristic form of government in all the Eastern civilizations was absolute monarchy, divinely ordained; the Great King was the agent of the gods when not himself a god; and the characteristic position in the royal presence was prostration. Art and learning were devoted primarily to the service of the gods and the god-kings. The basic institutions were immune to rational criticism because they were not regarded as man-made, for man's own purposes. The ruling principle of obedience bred the virtues of patience and fortitude; it might appear as fervent devotion, in time it could lead to the wisdom of resignation or the holiness of renunciation; but it always looks slavish to us because it was not a free choice but an unreasoned obedience to an arbitrary authority. The rare spirits who adventured never proclaimed an ideal of free choice or adventure.

Emerging from this background, the Greeks appear extraordinarily clear-eyed. Somehow they developed a faith in Mind as the distinctive essence of man; they enthroned the power of reason by which man might hope to dispel mystery and order his own life. This faith by no means denied the gods, but in effect it emancipated man from absolute dependence on them, or on priestcraft. While demanding ritual attentions, the Olympian gods otherwise left their worshipers pretty much alone. In this relative freedom the Greeks went on to develop their distinctive ideal of culture, as the conscious cultivation of human nature, the conscious realization of man's own powers for the pursuit of truth, beauty, and goodness. In political life they refused to deify their rulers and sought to rationalize authority. They developed their characteristic *polis*, a republican city-state with man-made laws, in which government was a public affair. They became citizens, not subjects. Their public duty was obedience to law, not subservience to authority. Outside of Sparta, they never regarded unquestioning obedience as a primary virtue.

Since we have inherited such attitudes and beliefs, we are likely to take them for granted and not to realize how singular they once were; so I shall risk being tedious by rehearsing a few elementary examples. One is the statement of Thales: "All things are made of water." Although the Western calendar is dated (somewhat inaccurately) from the birth of Christ, this simple, erroneous statement of Thales was perhaps as important a turning point in our history. Had his conjecture been truer it would not have been more significant, or more astounding. It represented an effort of Mind, without the aid of oracle and in defiance of all tradition and common sense, to explain the universe in its given natural terms. Men had always explained it by myths, in supernatural terms—the gods had made everything so. Thales left out the gods. Later they could be put back, if need be, and they were; but meanwhile he was thinking for himself, looking for natural causes. His statement symbolized the birth of disinterested, rational inquiry— the emancipation of mind that Renan called "the only miracle in history." It heralded the beginning of natural philosophy and science, the revolution in thought that eventually, for better or worse, was to transform man's life on earth much more conspicuously than have the teachings of Christ.

As revolutionary was the simple statement made by Socrates when on trial for his life: "The unexamined life is not worth living." This principle heralded the beginning of the endless quest of self-knowledge. It represented another defiance of authority, of traditional piety, of the wisdom of the ancestor. It got Socrates into trouble, naturally. We are likely to forget that by the standards of respectable, God-fearing Greeks he *did* corrupt the youth of Athens. His principle is still a revolutionary one and will still get people into trouble; it is not calculated to make our youth popular with their parents, their neighbors, or perhaps even some of their teachers. For once men begin examining the ideas they live by, there is no telling what they will come out with—the only certainty is that respectable ideas are in jeopardy. Still, this is what freedom of thought means, and why it has been rare.

My last example is the inevitable one—the Funeral Oration of Pericles, cited in every textbook. This chestnut may be called the first manifesto of democracy. Pericles not only boasted that Athenians were free men, able to live exactly as they pleased; he argued that freedom was what had made Athens great. He defined it as freedom under law—a principle that has remained basic in our political tradition. He stated explicitly an assumption that is essential to a faith in democracy, but that has been forgotten by many Americans, even aside from the authorities on un-American activities. Pericles emphasized that Athens trusted its citizens. Unlike Sparta, he pointed out, it freely admitted aliens into the city, enforced no rigorous discipline, and allowed its citizens to live as they pleased because it trusted to their native spirit rather than to "system and policy," or in other words to security regulations.

At the end I shall return to this assumption, which is one of those debatable ideas. Meanwhile it brings up the serious shortcomings of Athenian democracy. The citizens of Athens were a small minority, outnumbered by their slaves; they could live freely because slaves did most of the hard, dirty work. They had no Bill of Rights protecting the individual against the state, no laws guaranteeing freedom of thought and speech; the execution of Socrates was quite legal, as he himself recognized. The city might have done better with more "system"; its institutions were weak, some of them even fantastic. And Athenian democracy failed in the crisis: Sparta won the war during which Pericles made his oration. It was in the aftermath of this failure that the Greeks took to systematic political philosophy, which by democratic standards included some pretty dubious philosophy. Plato worked out his ideal *Republic:* a bee-hive society, in which the common people were mere drones, with no voice whatever in their government, and which might have been designed by the Grand Inquisitor. In his *Laws*, Plato specifically proscribed freedom of thought and speech, stating principles that in effect justified the execution of his beloved teacher Socrates.

My immediate concern, however, remains the positive

contributions that the Greeks nevertheless made to the cause of freedom—and continued to make even after the failure of Athens. The thought of Plato himself was remarkably free, adventurous, wide-ranging, and on the whole reasonable in tone; to this day he has been the most influential philosopher in Western tradition. As the first thinker to work out a coherent theory of the State, he should remind us of Zimmern's remark, that the Greeks made the all-important contribution to political philosophy—they invented it. They gave us the very words *politics* and *philosophy*, and with them many other words that indicate how much in our thought and culture stems from them—such words as theology, ethics, logic, history, physics, aesthetics, comedy, and tragedy. And the failure of Athens, followed by more wars in which all the Greek city-states lost their independence, itself led to another bold leap in thought. Plato and Aristotle never got beyond the little, self-sufficient *polis* in their thinking; their main object was to keep it small and self-sufficient. But when Alexander the Great became master of the Greek world and proceeded to conquer the Persian Empire, he conceived a wholly new kind of empire—a commonwealth in which the conquered peoples were to be partners rather than subjects. At a great banquet, during which representatives of all these peoples drank from a mixing bowl, Alexander offered a prayer for "a union of hearts." He was the first known man in the Western world to have this vision of brotherhood, several centuries before Christ. In the great world he opened up to the Greeks, the Stoic philosophers proceeded to rationalize his prayer. They formulated the ideal of a *cosmopolis*, a universal commonwealth, "one great City of gods and men." When St. Paul came to Athens on his missionary journey he quoted the Stoic Cleanthes, that all men are the offspring of God, as elsewhere he echoed the idea of Zeno, the founder of Stoicism, that God "dwelleth not in temples made with hands."

This Stoic ideal of *cosmopolis* prepared the way for the major Roman contribution to our political tradition —Roman law. Gradually built up under the Empire, Roman law approached a kind of universal common law; but long before this Cicero, under the influence of Greek philosophy, gave the classic statement of the ideal principles that became the guiding principles of the greater Roman emperors. His ideal Republic was a state representing the literal meaning of the word *republic:* a "public thing," the property of the people. More specifically, he described it as "an association or partnership in Justice." Justice he defined as a universal principle based on a law of Nature, an immutable law behind all actual laws and above mere custom: a law applying equally to all men, known by Right Reason, and universal because all men possess reason.

Now aside from the fact that the Roman Empire in practice fell far short of this lofty principle, there are obvious objections to the principle even in theory. One has only to ask, *name* one of these natural laws, or what do you mean by "Nature." There is in fact no such universally recognized law; "right reason" has justified quite different principles and practices, depending on culture and customs; and liberals have insisted on the importance of recognizing that law is not immutable, so that it may be freely changed to meet changing conditions. Nevertheless I gather that the principle of natural law is gaining favor again today among students of law. I think that most of us appeal to something like it when we condemn, for example, the ancient institution of slavery. We do not actually believe that slavery is merely a matter of custom or opinion, expedience or utility; we believe in our hearts that it simply isn't *right*. In any case my concern here is not the validity of the idea of natural law but its historical consequences. It can be a conservative force, a means of sanctifying the status quo. But chiefly it worked to promote the cause of freedom. Western thinkers derived from natural law the idea of natural rights, the rights of man as man, which the ancients had neglected. Among the plainest examples is our Declaration of Independence, beginning with its appeal to the "laws of nature and nature's God," and arguing therefrom that all men are equally entitled to life, liberty, and the pursuit of happiness.

Here I am brought to my second major topic, the actual influence of the classical tradition. In the Middle Ages, the dawn of Western civilization, the most conspicuous sign of this influence was the brilliant renaissance of the twelfth century, due to the partial recovery of classical thought and learning, which inspired something like the Greek faith in the power of reason. Bernard of Chartres acknowledged the debt to the ancients in his well-known saying, "We are like dwarfs seated on the shoulders of giants." But all along the dwarfs had preserved the memory of Roman law, and with it the ideal theory of the Roman state. Medieval thinkers kept asserting that the community was the source of political authority, that a primary object of such authority was justice, and that the authority was therefore limited by law. In this view, the king was the servant of the community, bound by law. Kings who thought otherwise found other medieval thinkers to support them, since a different view could also be justified by Roman theory and practice. Some jurists had written that the emperor had absolute legislative authority, some emperors had declared that they were above the law, and the Romans had never established any legal or constitutional means of holding the emperor to the law. Nevertheless, the idea persisted that kings must obey the law.

Such ideas might now be justified by Christian principles that went beyond the classical tradition. The great prophets of Israel had often defied its kings, in the name of the law of God, or in the interest of the poor and needy; some expressed an indignation over social injustice that was rarely voiced by the brilliant Greeks and the grave Romans. Implicit in the law of God was a principle of spiritual equality that held the germs of the idea of natural rights. The Greek *polis*, based on slavery, had never recognized a principle of equality, nor had the Roman Empire realized it in political practice; with the Stoics it remained a pretty abstract concept. That this Christian principle was a live idea in the Middle Ages, and a potential force, was indicated by the peasant rebellions. There had never been any such popular uprisings in ancient Egypt, Mesopotamia, or most of the Oriental sacred monarchies.

Yet these rebellions also make plain that medieval society was by no means a free society. The community, which in theory was the source of political authority, was neither in theory nor in practice based on principles of liberty or equality; it was a fixed hierarchy, with a mass of serfs at the bottom. Medieval thinkers, including St. Thomas Aquinas, justified serfdom or even slavery by the natural depravity of man, in particular of common men; common men were fit only to obey. Medieval thought was essentially authoritarian and absolutist, opposed on principle to freedom of thought and conscience, permitting no dissent on fundamentals; heresy was the worst of crimes. And Christian tradition could readily support political absolutism. St. Paul had said plainly that the powers that be are ordained by God, and that therefore any resistance to these powers would mean damnation; apparently it did not occur to him that if despotic powers were overthrown by other powers, God would presumably have to ordain these new powers too. The Christian Emperor Justinian who codified the Roman law had most emphatically asserted his superiority over it, and had required his officials to swear loyalty to him as a "divine and pious despot." The Byzantine Empire had returned under Christian auspices to the Oriental sacred monarchy—to the principles of miracle, mystery, and authority. These were still the ruling principles of medieval society. My thesis remains that a major reason why they did not continue to dominate Europe was the recapture of the Greek legacy, the return of the Greek spirit, which was signaled by the Renaissance.

This Renaissance, once pictured as a glorious period, has been drastically discounted by recent historians, and made to look more or less disreputable. Some historians have emphasized that it was greedy, licentious, and corrupt; others that it was backward-looking, indifferent to science, devoted to the academic classicism that saddled literature and education for centuries; others that it was less original than the medieval renaissance of the twelfth century. At least one historian dismisses it as a mere fiction, invented by historians. Nevertheless, a profound change did come over Europe in these centuries, and it seems to me clear that its main effect was an emancipation of mind. At least this becomes clearer in a broad view of freedom. If one looks only to political freedom, the Renaissance was a setback; it saw the rise of tyrannies in Italy, of absolute monarchy all over Europe. But if one looks to intellectual freedom, or specifically to Renaissance thought and art, there is no mistaking the signs of a new spirit, a new energy born of new hopes. They are the familiar signs of growing naturalism, humanism, and individualism, alike reflecting a growing interest in the natural man in the natural world, a sense of the rich possibilities inherent in earthly life, an often extravagant confidence in man's powers, his "high estate," his "excellent dignity." The disappointment of these high hopes, and the pessimism it often induced, then intensified the growth of a critical, skeptical spirit —it did not lead to a return to the medieval faith. To appreciate the world of difference that the Renaissance made, one has only to turn from St. Thomas Aquinas and Dante to Machiavelli and da Vinci, Rabelais and Montaigne, Bacon and Shakespeare.

All this by no means represented a simple break with Christianity. One reason why Christianity has been so dynamic as well as flexible a religion is the tension created by its radical dualisms of body and soul, the temporal and the spiritual, and from these the radically opposed tendencies, the extremes of optimism and pessimism which it has embraced. It has taught that man is naturally depraved, a wretched creature cursed by Original Sin, and that he is nevertheless fit for an eternity of bliss with his heavenly Father; that the whole world was created just for his sake, and that he should despise or flee this world; that human history is intensely meaningful and purposeful, and that all that matters is the hereafter; that life is sacred and that it is vile. Like St. Paul, Christianity has meant all things to all men.

One might argue that the Renaissance was a natural development of the humanistic tendencies in Christianity, and that the whole change that came over Europe would have happened anyway, with or without a classical tradition. I think it conceivably might have, given all those busy, energetic, worldly bourgeois. But there is no need of conjecturing about the actuality of the classical influence. The leading artists and humanists of the early Renaissance all testified to it in their enthusiasm over classical art and thought, as had Bernard of Chartres. The enthusiasm was most pronounced in Florence, the main center of the early Renaissance, and the most republican of the Italian city-states. And though the enthusiasts misunderstood a great deal, they did get hold of the essentials of Greek humanism and rationalism. Unlike the intellectuals of the Moslem world, who some centuries before them had also been excited by the discovery of Greek thought and learning, they hung on to the Greek spirit of free, critical inquiry. It was a spirit that they could hardly have caught from the Bible, any more than the Moslems could find warrant for it in their authoritarian Koran. In this spirit Westerners went on to new adventures in thought, notably the great advance in science, which grew out of Greek philosophy and science, and which in turn promoted the conscious ideal of intellectual freedom; while Islam returned to its Koran and settled into long centuries of intellectual torpor. In Europe itself still more striking evidence was provided by Czarist Russia. Russia had no Renaissance, caught nothing at all of the Greek spirit; it remained true to its Holy Orthodox faith, obedient to its Church and its czar; and so it remained a despotic state, uncontaminated by any ideal of freedom—political, intellectual, or religious —until it came under secular Western influence.

After the rise of science the Western world went ahead pretty much on its own steam. The direct influence of the Greeks became more or less incidental, and the most apparent influences were no longer liberating. Aristotle, for instance, became something of an intellectual nuisance; in the authoritarian Christian tradition he had been made an authority such as he had never been in the Greek world. In political thought he was chiefly a conservative influence; thinkers made most of his distrust of democracy and common men (though men of property are apt to come on such ideas all by themselves). Yet all along classical culture remained a living part of our tradition, as is demonstrated throughout this book, even cropping out in such unexpected places as the façades of Midwestern county courthouses. We are likely to forget that until this century most educated men in the Western world were brought up on the classics, and that many writers and thinkers have testified to the inspiration they got from them. In 1957 Albert Camus, when awarded the Nobel prize, told reporters that he had been "intellectually formed" by the Greeks.

As a final illustration of my main thesis, I shall cite the famous Lord Acton, who in the last century devoted most of his life and his vast learning to a projected History of Liberty that he never wrote, and that has been called the greatest book that was never written. I have gone through the notes he accumulated for it—many thousands of cards—and learned from them that one reason why he failed to write it was precisely the issue I am dealing with. At once a devout Catholic and an ardent Liberal, Lord Acton believed that the growth of Liberty was the main theme of all human history, and that Progress was Providence, God's plan for man; he wanted to believe that Christianity had been the main source of Liberty, and was still its mainspring; but he was forever troubled by the historic record of Christianity, in particular of his own Church, and by his awareness that historical Liberalism had not been primarily Christian, but largely even irreligious. So he went round and round the same worried circle, taking thousands of notes on such subjects as the medieval Papacy and the Inquisition, which got him nowhere in his History of Liberty. He was never able to concentrate on the secular sources of freedom often indicated in his notes: the rise of science, of rationalism, of skepticism—of a spirit that had originated in ancient Greece.

We may also regret that he was mistaken in his congenial belief that freedom is the central theme of man's whole history. Actually, freedom became a major theme only with the rise of the Greeks, and then again in later Western history. It was not a major theme in the ancient East, or in later China and India. On the face of the historical record, we can hardly say that man has a natural passion for freedom; for the overwhelming majority of men have not enjoyed it, or apparently missed it very much. The record suggests that the Grand Inquisitor was right, and that what most men really want or need is miracle, mystery, and authority.

Greco-Roman history forces this issue too. We have to face the fact that Athenian democracy failed in the crisis, that the Greeks lost their independence. After Alexander the Great, they were again ruled by kings, who had themselves deified, in the ancient Oriental manner. The Hellenistic kings were followed by Roman emperors, who were also made into gods. It seems unlikely that most Greeks and Romans literally believed in the divinity of their rulers, but in any case they accepted the forms of the Oriental sacred monarchy. When the Roman Empire became Christian it was ruled by absolute monarchs, who presently wore halos in their official portraits, and who required prostration in the royal presence. Long before this the slow decline in Greek philosophy had set in, beginning a century or so after Alexander the Great. Philosophy became less and less a critical inquiry, more and more a pursuit of peace of mind, then a cult of salvation by magical means. Greek religion and philosophy alike ended in a riot of Oriental superstition. The whole story may be summed up as a return to miracle, mystery, and authority.

Now the failure of the Greeks, in the first historic adventure in the free, open society, is hardly surprising. These "ancients" were only bright youngsters, with no long tradition to guide and settle them, and with nothing like our material and intellectual resources—our wealth and power, our knowledge and experience. In spite of our advantages, including the benefit of their experience, we are not too sure of our own prospects, even short of atomic war. The return of the irrational has been a major development of this century. It suggests a fear of freedom, an escape from freedom—from the burden of responsibility, in an open society that forces choices, and in a universe that leaves men alone. It is an open question whether men at large can maintain under stress the frame of mind and the habits of

thought essential to the maintenance of a free society.
Here, as I see it, is the basic issue. In the light both of
Christian and democratic idealism we can point to specific shortcomings of the Greeks and Romans that help
to explain their failure, for example their unconcern
about the poverty and ignorance of the masses, and their
blindness to the economic as well as moral evil of slavery;
but the issue finally comes down to the question of the
nature and potentialities of man, his fitness for freedom.
While the Greeks had many different things to say on
this as on all other questions, the living faith that made
possible their extraordinary achievements was a kind of
faith in man that Christians would come to describe as
the deadly sin of pride.

As the inventors of Tragedy, the Greeks were scarcely
optimists about man and his destiny. They had a sufficient sense of evil, which was fed by tragic experience,
and they never had the unique modern faith in progress.
Their thought is a healthy antidote to the excesses of
modern liberal optimism, which typically has lacked the
tragic sense of life. Nevertheless Greek tragedy, as I read
it, is an affirmation of the power and the dignity of the
human spirit, not a counsel of mere submissiveness or
humility. However reverent or fearful of the gods, the
Greeks continued to bank on man's own powers, his
capacities for the pursuit of truth, goodness, and beauty.
Homer had taught them that man could maintain his
own ideal values in defiance of mortality, or even of the
gods. Socrates spoke of heeding the voice of the daemon
within him, or what we might call the voice of God; but

the ideal he died for was the pursuit of wisdom and righteousness on earth, not the service of God or salvation in a life to come, and in his teaching it was an ideal that man could attain by his own efforts, without the grace of God. So was the good life according to Plato. Aristotle went further, asserting that Pride was "the crown of the virtues" and warning against undue humility, as both "commoner and worse" than vanity. Even the Stoics, with their sad wisdom of resignation and their ideal of freedom from all desire, were still proud; for they still taught that men could attain their freedom by their own powers of reason and will, without supernatural aid. And at the end even the Neo-Platonic mystics, taking off on the flight "from the alone to the Alone," got there by the powers of the human spirit, still proud of a feat that required no special gift of divine grace.

It was this attitude in particular that St. Paul branded as the foolishness of the Greeks. Paul knew what the ,Church Fathers and St. Augustine taught after him, that man can know nothing and achieve nothing except by the grace of God. Medieval churchmen and the Protestant Reformers continued to emphasize man's utter dependence on such grace, more especially as a creature of Original Sin; they naturally believed that the only hope for him lay in discipline and authority, not in freedom. This was the dominant Christian tradition until the Renaissance. With the Renaissance there returned the Greek faith in man's own powers, and following the rise of science there grew up the novel faith in progress, which enabled Lord Acton to believe that progress was the law of God. But with the crisis of our times the old Christian tradition has revived. Reinhold Niebuhr brands the faith in progress as the sin of pride, the root evil of our time. In England Herbert Butterfield, whose book *Christianity and History* appears to have made a considerable impression, calls the faith in human nature a "disastrous heresy." In the most fashionable literary quarters there is much talk of Original Sin.

Now I doubt that harping on the theme of Original Sin helps very much, either in understanding men or getting them to behave better—they behaved badly enough in the Middle Ages. But in any case it hardly promotes the cause of freedom, any more than it did in the Middle Ages. I should insist that one who cherishes freedom *must* risk the "disastrous heresy" of faith in human nature. If man is essentially corrupt and depraved, he is simply not fit for freedom, and there can be no hope for a free society. One who believes in democracy must go further and risk the faith expressed by Pericles in the native spirit of ordinary Athenians, the sufficient good sense and good will of common men; for if only security regulations can prevent Americans from being corrupted by subversive influences, there is no security for American democracy. Finally one may venture an answer to the Grand Inquisitor. It does not appear that man has an innate passion for freedom; but at least there is reason to believe that men who have been brought up in freedom do cherish it, and would not knowingly, willingly, give it up. The Greek cities struggled for centuries to maintain what independence they could. The lights in the classical world went out very slowly, and at that never did go out altogether.

Even on religious grounds it would seem reasonable to invest faith in a creature who was reputedly created in the image of God. But I think that those who argue that we can maintain our hopes for a free society only on a Christian basis need to consider our history a little more deeply—and also to consider the attitudes of some eminent religious historians today. Thus Arnold Toynbee has viewed very calmly the prospect of the collapse of our civilization, since he regards it, in the words of St. Paul, as merely a "vain repetition of the heathen"—of the pride of the Greeks; he has grown more hopeful lately only because he thinks that the probable loss of our political and economic freedoms might lead to more "spiritual" freedom. Herbert Butterfield points out that Christians have less reason than others to worry about the future, or to fear a new kind of society, for under any kind of tyranny they would always have something to live for—they would always have Christ. He concluded his *Christianity and History* with this message: "Hold to Christ, and for the rest be totally uncommitted."

Well, I see no necessity, once more, of choosing between the Greeks and Christ. It is possible to hold' to both. My point is simply that most of us want to hang on to our freedoms too, that we thereby *are* committed to some other earthly values, and that for these values we are deeply indebted to the classical legacy.